The Miracle on Corcoran Street

The Memoir of a Man Whose Life Was Guided by Nuns, Prostitutes, and Other Surrogate Mothers

Dr. James A. Anderson

ISBN 978-1-952315-619

Library of Congress Cataloging - 2024904501

The Miracle on Corcoran Street: The Memoir of a Man Whose Life Was Guided by Nuns, Prostitutes, and Other Surrogate Mothers/
Dr. James A. Anderson

1. Literary Collections–Non-Fiction

2. Non-Fiction-Memoir

3. Non-Fiction-Inspirational

Printed in the United States of America

Table of Contents

DEDICATION

This memoir is dedicated to Mother Mary E. Lange, a Black Catholic nun who in 1829 founded the U.S. first African religious congregation, the Oblate Sisters of Providence in Baltimore, MD (Saint Frances Academy). Their mission was to help the "poor and neglected" inner-city Black children. She and her congregation of nuns sought to counter the racial, social, and religious context of the Catholic Church which existed at a time of slavery and marginalization of communities of color. The Oblate Sisters were trailblazers who persevered despite being overlooked or suppressed by those who resented or disrespected them, and who ignored the education of Black children.

From kindergarten thru the 4th grade I was educated, protected, and cared for by the Oblate sisters at St. Augustine's elementary school in Washington, DC. They successfully competed for my soul with the Ledroit Park Gang who groomed young boys to become gang members who engaged in nefarious activities. My success in life has resulted from the cocoon of protection and the positive values that the nuns provided as they worked with Black prostitutes and other community groups to support Black children.

In 2023 Pope Francis, the leader of the Catholic Church, recognized Marie Lange for her heroic virtue and nominated her for "sainthood". With the paucity of Black and female saints this was a monumental step forward. A critical component of advancing toward sainthood is evidence that the candidate performed a miracle, which should be viewed in the context of a candidate's historical efforts. Marie Lange and the Oblate Sisters were committed to the education and support of Black children in poor communities.

My life is an example of the product they produced, in other words, "I AM THE MIRACLE" that Marie Lange and the Oblate sisters produced with God's blessing.

INTRODUCTION

It has taken me six years to understand that **MY VOICE MATTERS, MY STORY MATTERS**, and **MY TRUTH MATTERS.**

Were it not for those who encouraged me to share this incredible story, I undoubtedly would not have written it. Authors pen their memoirs for varied reasons and some reach deep into their psyche to identify both content & context. For years I was hesitant to write the first word – fearful that I would relive forgotten traumas, fragmented memories, and confirm my long-held beliefs that the absence of love, affection, and security underscored my troubled emotional past.

Yet, it was that past which provided the strength that I needed to survive and become successful. I have attempted to reconcile the fact that for five decades across professional educational landscapes, I was considered an expert and/or champion on those aspects of student learning (K-16, that were impacted by culture, race, class, gender, and diversity Yet, I am still the fearful little boy searching for his roots, for answers, and for a mother's love. While writing this memoir, I have lost and found parts of myself I never knew existed. In retrospect, my life has appeared to be a movie.

It began as a drama full of doubt, fear, bravado, and little love. At eleven years old, I began to experience a stream of events that would set the stage for a life-long, intense search for my personal existential meaning. This memoir is not just a historical reflection, rather I am trying to write, authentically, through a traumatized lens – a lens which has repeatedly shaped both my memory and my psyche. Hopefully, my words will free others who have been locked into the past for decades.

The choice of my professional career as a psychologist was influenced to a great degree by the gaps in my emotional memory and my longing for closure. Did that professional decision make a difference? Yes, in the sense that I learned theories, concepts, terms, and explanations that provided intellectual insight, but I still had few emotional answers, thus it took the efforts of close friends, relatives, and key figures to buffer my enduring sadness.

An example of intellectual insight was reflected in my overreliance upon the psychological technique of compartmentalization. This defense mechanism allows one to place his/her most prominent fears, anxieties, and emotional difficulties into different "compartments" in their psyche. Quite simply, it is a subconscious avoidance technique. Throughout this memoir, certain themes will be evident. Some, like spirituality, I still struggle with. As I aged, the presence of caring mentors was instrumental in terms of my critical life decisions.

The mentors influenced my journey to and through some of the finest universities in the country where I emerged as a senior administrator, and ultimately as a university Chancellor (President). My adult life has been a commitment to surviving and thriving in educational settings, yet my early life outside of that setting, especially in the streets, provided the strength and resilience that carried me into and through my adult professional endeavors.

I did not realize for decades how the absence of a linear relationship between my early years and my adult years would impact my unconscious psyche and identity development. Consequently, I developed a dual persona that I have folded into my total being. The following chapters will carry the reader through the first half of my incredible life journey.

The concept of 'fear' has played out in a dualistic manner throughout my life. For the longest time, I feared to commit intensely to personal relationships, yet as I matured, I never feared confronting complex problems or difficult individuals in my professional life.

A consistent and most critical theme speaks to my evolution as a Black man, in multiple scenarios involving multiple players. Sometimes those interactions were antagonistic and even dangerous, and other episodes were rewarding and resulted in positive results. At different points in my life several negative experiences involved white males in authority and shaped my perceptions of them and my future interactions with them.

I attended a prominent white high school, an elite White university as an undergraduate, and earned a Ph.D. from an Ivy League university. I was a VP and President at four different universities, but what mattered was that I was often treated abusively because I was Black. I would venture to say that a significant percentage of Black and Hispanic men beyond the age of 50 years can recall similar experiences; Many have revealed this to me. The most consequential theme that permeates my early memories involves the unconditional support that I received from the angels of humanity – women. I am scared to think of what I would have become without their intervention (probably prisoner # 4791335).

I do not know why I was chosen by a higher power to be blessed by these angels, but I do know that their motivation was due to their inherent goodness. As I emerged into manhood and beyond, what stood out was their ability to continue to love me and care for me when my distrust and fear of abandonment caused me to hurt them or disappoint them. I have stood my ground in their defense as well as all Black people, other groups of color, and White allies.

Women are the JEWELS of the universe, but I cannot understand why God has chosen them and their children to suffer so much throughout history. I must be truly blessed to have been one of the chosen ones who was led through the sometimes-dark pathways of life to ultimately survive. This memoir represents a final summary attempt to fill in the gaps and to connect the disarrayed pieces of the puzzle of my early life.

I have talked with God or some omnipotent being (no answer yet), beseeched him/her, doubted, and cursed him/her and gave thanks. I fell in love with the virgin Mother Mary when she saved my life and that of my mentally challenged daughter, and I have stayed true to my devotion to her. I struggled to co-exist as an emerging young thug and a good Catholic boy. I have yet to resolve my anger and disgust with a Catholic Church that historically has protected priests who were/are sexual predators. I will describe my encounter with one of Satan's infantry while I served as an altar boy in one of Christ's churches.

As I write this memoir, at times, I feel that I am exhaling, and in doing so, I am experiencing a long and deep expulsion of breath and emotion unlike anytime I can remember. I do not know what to expect when I finish this catharsis, but then I have not been good at predicting many outcomes in my life. I hope that for me, and others like me, this becomes my/their Book of Revelations. I simply want to know why my parents chose to abandon me and why after six decades they have never come to look for me. I have been blessed with intellect and a critical eye, yet I often cannot answer the most fundamental questions about my life.

I am hoping that by putting my life into print, I can remove some of the pain, sadness, and occasional rage that I have allowed to burden my existence. I had no parent to teach me right or wrong during my formative years but I had a passion – MY SURVIVAL AND THE PROTECTION OF THE YOUNG WOMAN THAT I THOUGHT WAS MY REAL SISTER.

This memoir will not cover my entire life, instead it will cover from birth thru graduate school (roughly 29 years). This represents the time-period during which my personality, identity, major values, beliefs, and biases were formed and solidified. I am fully aware that my professional adult life has also been influenced in different ways by the same factors that I describe in this memoir, but my core personality developed in those first twenty-nine years that did not involve working in professional settings. Perhaps at some point I will cover that latter period. Many of my early years were influenced by my relations with Catholic nuns, neighborhood prostitutes, and gang members.

Will writing this book end my varied periods of grief? The grip of disillusionment may never completely disappear, but at least I may be able to address certain absolutes that have dominated my psyche and my life. Among these is the burdensome belief that I could not place absolute trust in anyone, and secondarily, praying to alter one's life circumstances is like playing the lottery. The chances that your prayers will be answered are slim or none.

One of the most poignant summations of my life was provided by a news reporter who interviewed me while I served as a Vice President at the State University of New York at Albany (2006-2008):

"James Anderson's life story is the sort of tale that, if you read it in a book, would prompt you to say, "That can't be true. Who thinks up this stuff?"[1]

---

[1] Deborah Moore, Special to the Times Union (newspaper) Albany, NY. June 25th, 2006

CHAPTER 1
A TRAUMATIC BEGINNING

I was seven years old and had just arrived at the elementary school that morning with my sister. As the other students filed into the classroom, Peggy and I asked the Catholic nun if we could speak to her privately.

The nuns at St. Augustine's elementary school in NW Washington, D.C. had successfully developed a secure rapport with the students over time, hence we felt comfortable talking to her.

"What's the issue children?" sister asked.

"We have not seen our caretaker, Mrs. Dawson, for four days. We get up in the morning and she is not there. When we get home from school, she is not there, and when we go to sleep, she is not there. We don't have any food and we are scared."

"Have you called any relatives to let them know?"

"We don't know who to call."

"We don't have any relatives." I responded.

"All right, let's walk down to the principal's office."

Peggy and I were afraid because the principal, Sister (Mother Consolata, usually seemed so stern.

"Sister Joan Francis said that you have not seen Mrs. Dawson for a few days, is that true?" asked Sister Consolata.

"Yes, sister, and we are really hungry."

She picked up the phone and spoke to someone and then turned to us and spoke, "Go down to the lunchroom and Mrs. Brown will give you some breakfast.

When you finish, go straight to your classroom. I mean straight to your classroom. Do you understand? I will check on the issue with Ms. Dawson."

"Yes sister, thank you."

For the rest of the day a million scenarios ran through my mind and most were not positive. At the end of the class day Sister Joan Francis approached Peggy and I.

"Would you both walk with me next door to the convent?"

"Yes sister," we responded.

When we arrived and walked in, Sister Consolata was there, and she asked us to sit down next to her on the couch and began to speak softly:

"I want you two to remember that sometimes difficult things happen in our lives, but God loves us and will always protect us."

At that moment I knew we were going to hear some bad news. Sister Consolata continued, "We have learned that Ms. Dawson has passed away." Confused, I said

"But when is she coming home, we miss her." Sister realized that we did not understand the concept "passed away."

"My sweet children, Mrs. Dawson is now with the angels because she has died."

Peggy and I burst into tears, and I screamed, "Why didn't someone tell us before now? What are we going to do now, we don't have anyone now."

From that point on everything changed and I realized that the first adult anchor in my life was now gone. I could have tumbled into a deep depression, but instead, I simply shut out most of the world then, and did so even more when, years later, I was separated from my sister in a very cold, dispassionate way.

I regret that I was not given the opportunity to say goodbye to Mrs. Dawson – The first angel in my life. What do you call a childhood that was devoid of attention, affection, love, security, and parents?

What results when a child was deprived of birthday celebrations, the joys of Christmas, and the communal warmth of Thanksgiving and other family gatherings? What do you call a childhood that made a boy, a man-child at seven years old, yet as he grew older, he longed to be the child he was not allowed to be. In short, you call it MY LIFE. My childhood was an enigmatic blur, a motion picture with no credits at the end, and it both went too fast and seemed too long.

My childhood was a crude flashbulb of memories that are not connected by any short or long threads of continuity, and those memories also are too few to construct a realistic story. While searching to find some semblance of meaning during the early years of my childhood, I was drawn to the unpredictable yet attractive alluring streets of Washington, DC. and the neighborhood gang to meet my basic needs, and for protection.

Simultaneously, I was delivered (by whom?) to an order of Catholic nuns and local prostitutes who joined forces to guide me, keep me out of trouble, socialize me, and encourage me to dream and have hope. I was the link that brought both groups together with a common purpose.

As an adult I learned over time to understand so much more about both groups as caring, loving, and dedicated women, and their intrinsic motivation was to nurture to the degree that they could. Moreover, there was never any hesitation in their motivation to support me. To this day, the concept of "prostitute" represents to me caring women who were conned by men to adopt a lifestyle that would grow the men's income. Even though this sounds like a generalization, I was the recipient of their love and concern; hence, I bring personal evidence that allows me to generalize.

I must also honor the woman who was inspired to take me home from the hospital rather than have me sent to an orphanage or be placed in foster care. I was abandoned by my birth mother shortly after my delivery and my early years were spent in the care of Ms. Dawson. I knew that she was a caretaker and not my mother. During these years, another child was present in my life and I was raised to believe that we were sister and brother.

Try as I might, I cannot remember Mrs. Dawson's first name, nor do I remember my sister Peggy's last name. I was told decades ago that Mrs. Dawson was the elevator operator at the hospital where I was born, and her caring heart did not want me to enter situations of unpredictable or possibly depraved care, hence, she took me home. The plight of many black children since slavery was often in the hands of those who were responsible for their care, even though the adults may not be family nor have a legal context for raising that child. I presume that she also rescued Peggy although I am not sure of the circumstances.

The depth of this story will be shared with you in subsequent chapters. I only ask that you accept and tolerate the gaps in storytelling that I cannot remember. I surmise that much of this was due to childhood and adolescent trauma that forced my emotion and attention to focus on sheer survival. Making sense of my world, and in that world, young females and adult women played the key roles in my survival, happiness, joy, and pain. Without them, my future would have been a darker cloud.

I can attest to the protective roles often assigned to women since I was provided with female guardians throughout my life, and I trust them much more than men in general. There are a few men that I learned to love and trust, and their importance cannot be understated, but they appeared later in life. My birth father has never been a part of my life. Why, I don't know. I do not even know if he was aware of my existence and his paternity.

Thus, I have no memories of interacting or playing with someone I could identify as "my father." I don't even know his damn name, my mother's name, or my real name. As you will learn in later chapters, my current name is a product of both a fabricated birth certificate and a legal formal petition for adoption which was entered while I was a college student.

I attempted several times to put my early life into print, but I often became overwhelmed with sadness as I wrote, hence, I stopped. Over the years, I have been encouraged by many who are close to me, and who love and care about me to share how I overcame trauma to live and to prosper. I have also been influenced by a book I read in college that still has personal meaning for me. It is called *Tally's Corner* by Elliot Liebow and it is a penetrating analysis of "Negro" men who hung out on a street corner in northwest Washington, DC in the 1960's.

Liebow found that the whole social structure of the street corner world rested, to a large extent, on the primary face-to-face relationships of personal networks. In a distorted way, this served as a sort of family for many of them, and many were brought into this family at a young age.

Talley's corner was seven blocks from the corner where I hung out, and most corners had a similar gathering of men. The young boys would listen to their lies, their stories, their boastful conquests. It was an indirect form of socialization for youthful black males, but the real rite of passage for me would come from direct interactions with the Ledroit Park Gang. The Park itself is not large, and it is located at 16th and Florida Avenue, but its influence and territorial control were vast. This book concerns my pursuit of meaning and belonging, and the persons who were central characters in my complex evolutionary play. While this book is my story; it is also a tribute to all poor and abandoned children who struggle(d) to survive and feel valued.

Moreover, it is a tribute to the women who cared about, loved, protected, educated, rescued, tolerated, and forgave me; they repeatedly opened the gates to the next stage of my manhood. I am forever grateful to all of you, and I sincerely apologize for those times when I failed you and disappointed you.

In retrospect, I know that for most of my life, you have been there when I needed you. This was crucial since, as a child and young male, I was not able to find answers, and not able to find a substitute for my sorrow, loneliness, and my constant search for meaning. You were there when I struggled as a man-child in an irrational world and uncompromising storm. I was protected by my angels. Someone once told me that my life was a true "ghetto to glory" story, but in retrospect that designation seems trite relative to the actual events and the roller coaster emotions that consumed my existence.

My decades of sorrow far outweighed any "glory" that I am due or deserve. Decades later, I still struggle annually on Mother's Day. Father's Day is less meaningful to me. Every Mothers' Day, I ponder a question repeatedly: "I wonder if she thinks about me today?" In my futility, I don't know what answer would truly satisfy me and bring some closure to the biggest hole in my storybook. To this day I beat myself up for not being able to share myself with those women who attempted to love me. My belief that most of my life was one big unhappy ending, interfered with my attempts to love and be loved.

CHAPTER 2
CHILDHOOD MEMORIES

I think that I chose the academic discipline of psychology as a career pathway because I lacked most childhood memories of people, events, and emotional connections. I had hoped that by immersing myself into the field of psychology, I would discover the story that answered the never-ending stream of my unresolved questions.

Among the important questions, was my concern about the absence of my parents at birth. My persistent belief as I became older was that I did something to drive them away, or something was wrong with me, and I was not worth being taken care of by them. I burdened myself with these and other thoughts for decades.

While pursuing my studies in college, I learned that memory in childhood is qualitatively and quantitatively different from memories formed in early or late adolescence and adulthood. As adults look back to childhood, we have great difficulty remembering things before the age of three or four.

Children can retain factual or fictional information but their brains are not developed enough to form information into complex bundles which become the linkages we need for memory. While I possess an excellent long-term memory for thousands of events and people since my teen years, I lack a mental camera for many personal experiences and people within the first ten years of my life.

This condition is known as aphantasia and it refers to the "mind's eye" that people may lack. Many individuals in this situation cannot visually replay or relive traumatic experiences. In retrospect, it appears that from birth to my early teens, my cultural memory outweighed other types of personal, incident-based memories. My cultural memory was influenced by events in my cultural milieu, especially my participation in groups that had a profound effect on me or were sources of protection (actual or perceived).

I desperately wish that I could remember who told me, and when they told me, that my birth was the unholy product of date rape. Purportedly, my mother was freshman in college and went on a date with a sailor who got her drunk and raped her. A seminal question that has haunted me is what occurred in the moments after I was born.

Long ago, I created two possible scenarios that I fantasized could have happened:

Scenario 1

I assumed at birth that I was placed in my mother's secure arms. I hope she spoke lovingly to me as she gazed into my eyes. Perhaps she was successful in her attempts to breastfeed her little treasure: my first meal and the attachment dynamic began to develop. The nurses surrounded the bed and, although they used different words, they assured my mother that I am, absolutely, a beautiful gift.

I fall asleep after my belly is full of breast milk, and my mother does the same. The nurse lifts me from her arms, carries me into an adjoining room, and places me in a bassinet. The next day, my mother dresses me in a cute blue outfit and she sits down in a wheelchair with me in her arms. Her parents and her brother, who attends the same university as her, roll her out of that room and down the hall to the office, where she places my name on a birth certificate and shares the name of the absent father.

In essence, she documents that I am her son, and that I belong to her. I remember the tactile feeling of my little hand grasping her finger. Her gaze and her smile offered comfort and security. To someone else, I had value and worth.

Scenario 2

The glow that my mother felt after my birth, after holding me and breastfeeding me, is challenged as she begins to argue with her parents. The point of contention concerns whether my mother will take me home the next day.

Her parents remind her that weeks before, during a serious discussion about her future, my mother agreed that trying to raise an infant while attending college was not feasible. Moreover, her parents would not accept that stain on the family's reputation due to her giving birth out of wedlock.

In this scenario, my real father probably told my mother several times that he was not able to provide for me, and he wanted no part of her pregnancy, nor did he want to be with her at all. During the last weeks of her pregnancy, he completely severed contact.

Despite this antagonistic discussion with her parents, my mother had fallen in love with her new baby, and she was determined to keep me. She and her parents were totally against an abortion. The deciding factor was that her parents stated they would not support her while raising this child and would continue to support, financially, her remaining years of college.

My mother acquiesced. Unfortunately, she believed that I would be adopted and that my story would end well. Thus, she kissed me goodbye and left with her parents. My future would now begin with no parents, no grandparents, and, in essence, no blood family and it would stay that way to this day. What good is life with no real family and no anchors? Where was God?

I have no idea if either scenario is true. Most likely, there are aspects of reality and romanticism that may conjoin. Early in life, I created many scenarios that reflected alternate realities, and I'm sure they served some purpose for me at that time. Alternate realities can be based upon facts, devoid of facts, or, in my case, can be a combination of wishes, dreams, and some facts. I have been searching for a sense of wholeness. Perhaps, the scenarios represent puzzle pieces from the past that I created to add a more complete picture of who I am. This seemed necessary, otherwise I would have a big empty hole in my existence and a crushing depression would follow. I recognize the possibility that both scenarios may be false, but I lacked a viable alternative.

Note that in scenarios 1 and 2, my mother did hold me after birth. I probably have been afraid to contemplate a possible scenario 3 in which she left the hospital without any physical contact at all. In other words, she simply gave birth and, for whatever reasons, she wanted no contact or emotional relationship with her child.

In this scenario, I was not bathed in the infant protection that accompanies a mother's touch, and the critical value of this specific tactile stimulation is well-documented as important to healthy infant development. There is a linkage between childhood trauma, amnesia and ultimately memory, and it is apparent to me that I have buried many memories of my childhood.

To a great degree my life has been a reaction to harm done starting at birth into early adolescence. In her book, *Free From Lies: Discovering Your True Needs*, author Alice Miller says, "By denying that you were unloved as a child, you will spare yourself some pain, but you also block the path to your own truth. This love we were hoping for as children is not waiting for us. It was never there, and it will never be there." I am afraid to think that this might be true.

How can I not think of my early existence as worthless to my real mother and father? Later in her book, Alice Miller continues, "An unwanted child's desperate struggle for the right to live begins in the womb, leading later to a loss of the capacity to love and trust others, and (in some cases) an inevitable inclination toward self-destructiveness." That is where I was headed, I presumed that my life would not end well. The adult equivalent to my situation is when a person suffers from PTSD (post-traumatic stress disorder) and may or may not remember the trauma that caused the amnesia. After much research and reflection, I have identified several sources of my childhood trauma:

1) absence of parents,
2) emotional neglect,
3) stress caused by the conditions of poverty, and
4) other actual traumatic events.

The loss of memory for months, years, and decades can be both jarring and feel as if one is suspended in an empty jar. I have spent decades attempting to identify a rhythm that links time periods, events, and people. I now understand why people hold on to religion so dearly and desperately – it provides the

---

rhythm that can connect the past, the present, and hopes for the future. That rhythm may not be realistic, but it serves its purpose for many.

My loneliness and lack of familial connections translated into verbally targeting many friends. To make matters worse, I attempted to cover up my cruel behavior by feigning that I was joking. I learned to appreciate the strength of my victims who continued to tolerate my hurtful words and maintain a close friendship. They could have easily dismissed me from their lives. My pain insulated me from accepting and loving many who tried to bring out the best in me.

CHAPTER 3
THE EARLY YEARS
(birth to 6 years old)

I was not raised by my birth parents, instead I was told that at birth, I was left at the hospital. I assume that the hope was that I would be placed in a foster home, orphanage or be adopted.

Decades ago, I heard a story that the elevator operator at the hospital decided to take me home, but I cannot remember who told me that. My rescuer's name was Mrs. Dawson and I simply cannot remember her first name. She was a beautiful older woman with silver-gray hair and a warm smile. Perhaps, I don't remember a lot about her because most of my time was spent either at school, in the streets begging for money, or hanging out with my friends. I had no restrictions at five, six, or seven years old because I was a man-child, who falsely believed he could take care of himself, and I often did.

We lived in a second-floor apartment at 1430 Corcoran Street, NW, nothing memorable, but it provided a roof over our head. It was located on a narrow, one-way street bounded on all sides by major thoroughfares: between R & S streets, NW and 14th & 15th streets, NW. When I was growing up in that area, the neighborhood was populated by minorities-primarily black folk. Today, gentrification has erased most of the color from that area and now whites predominate.

They bring no memory nor empathy of what was. Fourteenth street from U street to Florida Avenue, used to be a corridor serving humanity, but now it is nothing but a commercial corridor. There were two apartments' downstairs: one occupied by Mr. and Mrs. Russell and the other by an older white woman who liked to give me marshmallows. Mr. and Mrs. Russell were very nice to Peggy and me. One hot summer day, the couple took us to get ice cream. That was the first time any adult had shown Peggy and me any kind of attention other than the nuns and Mrs. Dawson. I remember one situation very clearly that involved Mr. Russell.

I was walking down the stairs from my second-floor apartment on my way to meet my friends. Midway, I stopped in my tracks because the landing that led to the exit door was colored white when normally it was dark brown.

"Mr. Russell, Mr. Russell help me I'm scared, what is wrong with the floor." He rushed out of his apartment, looked down at the floor and said, 'wow,' then he looked at me and smiled.

"Come here and let me carry you to the front door." I walked down a few steps, and he picked me up. "How did the floor become white overnight," I quizzically asked.

"It's not the color white, son, these are termites."

I had no idea what he was referring to. He continued,

"These are insects that like to eat wood." I scanned the floor again. "There's like a zillion of them, do you have a can of bug spray to kill them?"

He laughed again, "Bug spray does not kill them, we need a professional exterminator. I'll take care of that."

I exited the door and walked onto the sidewalk feeling very uneasy. The most unique feature of the external architecture of the edifice where I lived was a tunnel that led to the back of the apartment building. Over time, when we were being chased by the police or a rival gang, that tunnel became a sacred portal, and I or my crew of equally young boys would use it as an escape route to disappear into a labyrinth of alleyways, garages, and back yards. No other structure on the block possessed such odd architecture.

As I indicated earlier, living with Mrs. Dawson and me was a young female who appeared to be about a year older. Her name was Peggy, and I presumed her last name was also Dawson, given to her by Ms. Dawson. Peggy and I were just given this last name, but not legally. My earliest memory is that when the three of us were in that apartment, Ms. Dawson would give us baths together, I guess to lower the water bill, and we would play with a couple of small toy ships that we had.

The ships were small and cheap prizes from a cereal box. I do not remember possessing any real toys. Toys has always been a staple of a child's experience in many western cultures, but poverty deprived me of that treasure. I do remember Peggy and I at a toy store once and she saw a doll that she gushed over, but Mrs. Dawson could not afford to get it for her.

I presented Peggy with that doll a few days later. I had stolen it from the toy store, one of the only criminal acts of my early youth. Normally, I only stole food for the three of us. I would never let Peggy and Mrs. Dawson go hungry.

I told a Catholic nun once that I stole food so we could eat, and she responded harshly, "You know that is a sin don't you, and you could get arrested."

"Yes sister, I know both of those things, but God does not want his children to go hungry, does he?"

"No, he does not," she said. "What about getting caught?"

I laughed and responded, "Come on sister, the 'man' has too many other things to do rather than waste time arresting a young kid who is starving."

She gazed at me momentarily, "Just be careful, please. Sometimes when you don't have any food, just come to the convent, and we will give you some to take home." I remember they ate a lot of sweets like cakes.

Those baths were some of the happiest moments I can remember because they involved the three of us engaged in a caring moment. Mrs. Dawson found the energy to play with us, but she could never answer any questions about my real parents and family. I don't think she really knew much. Peggy and I were very protective of each other.

We walked to and from school every day and sometimes a few friends would accompany us. We were never afraid because kids in our neighborhood were under the watchful eye of the Ledroit Park gang who were alternately dangerous and protective. By the time that I was almost eight years old, I was being groomed to be a gang member, specifically a pimp, whatever that was. Peggy and I and our friends would eat lunch together at school.

One day, one of the students who tried to intimidate other students came to our table and demanded that we give him our lunch desserts. His name was Nathaniel. The only two things that I remember about him was that when he talked loud, spit would come out of his mouth, and he was very dark-skinned, like a piece of coal. For many kids like me, a negative association developed: a dark-skinned, loud-speaking intimidator or tormentor was trying forcibly to take something from us.

On this day, he zeroed in on me. I will never forget that day because Peggy became my (S)hero when she confronted Nathaniel, who was in the process of focusing his scare tactics on me. As he sat down next to me, I saw a fist fly by my face, barely grazing my nose, and land squarely on Nathaniel's jaw.

Peggy had just clocked him and she also said to him, "Get out of my brother's face and don't come over to our table again!"

I was witnessing a different side of her. She was sweet, but a warrior. The lunchroom fell silent waiting for Nathaniel to retaliate. The seconds that passed seemed like several minutes. Suddenly, I stood up as did my two male friends at the table David, and Peaches. We were sending a message to Nathaniel that it was now 4 to 1. At that moment, to other students who were watching, we were the new defense department, all around 7 to 8 years old. Nathaniel never bothered us again. I had just initiated my "rep" (reputation).

One other young boy at Saint Augustine's is etched in my memory: Leroy. He was a handsome, curly-haired, athletic ball of hypertension. His emotional outbursts were daily, but generally not directed at anyone. This made him unpredictable and sometimes scary.

I had an okay relationship with him for two reasons: I never criticized him or called him "crazy," like other students, or acted afraid of him; and I took the time to listen to him when he ranted. One day, as students milled around the playground at lunch, someone pointed to the top of the main building and shouted,

"Leroy is going to jump!"

He was there, pacing back and forth frantically and screaming that he was going to jump. This went on for about 20 minutes before a few police officers grabbed him and escorted him downstairs. Despite the efforts by the nuns to calm students, tension and fear hung thick in the air. In retrospect, I wondered what impulse drove him to consider jumping and how would the catholic nuns explain this traumatic event to the students to assuage their fears.

There was no question in my mind that Leroy was on the verge of jumping. I guess his pain and emotional distress felt constantly unbearable. I could identify with such distress, but not to that extreme. We never saw him again at school.

CHAPTER 4
THE OBLATE SISTERS OF PROVIDENCE

During my early years I attended Saint Augustine Elementary School in NW Washington, DC. The school was administered by an order of black catholic nuns, the students were all African-American, and it was situated in a predominantly black community.

Thus, my reality and my existence bore the color BLACK. The mission of the nuns stretched far beyond simply teaching. They connected with the external community and they were a security blanket for their beloved students. While administering to our educational and spiritual needs, the nuns assumed the roles of counselor, friend, confidant, mentor, and role- model. When necessary, they even exhibited a firm, no- nonsense parental posture that could send chills down a child's spine. They seemed familiar with the stark environment that many of the children woke up to every day.

Even though childhood depression does not manifest itself as it does in adolescence, the nuns sensed when one of us had not eaten, lacked proper clothes, or were emotionally troubled, and /or abused (emotionally or physically). Since they were the first order of Catholic nuns that I had interacted with, I assumed that there were many black nuns in Washington, DC and throughout the country. I knew nothing about the history of their order and their passion to educate black children, and to help us believe that a future was possible.

Several times, I have researched the origins of those black nuns and I learned that they were the Oblate Sisters of Providence and were the first successful Roman Catholic sisterhood in the world established by women of African descent. The order was founded in Baltimore, in 1828 by a group of four free Women of Color who had fled the turmoil of slave insurrections on the French Colony of Santa Domingo. The order was co-founded by a Sulpician priest, James Hector Joubert, a French refugee, and educator Elizabeth Clarisse Lange, a Caribbean refugee.

They met in Baltimore in 1828 and created a black religious community to educate black girls, a feat that challenged prevailing, social, and Episcopal attitudes about race, gender, and the stark racism of the Catholic Church and women's religious orders. Several decades later, they admitted young boys. A six-year-old does not understand such a proud history, nor was I exposed to it.

All I knew was that I felt encouraged and protected in the nun's presence. The Oblate Sisters demanded a certain standard of excellence in the classroom, and if they surmised that a student was academically gifted, they demanded more. I was in that category, and as a result, the nuns gave me responsibilities outside the classroom. At times, I felt that they unfairly demanded more of me than other students. A few of the nuns admitted that was the case, but they explained why it was necessary to prepare me for a difficult future, when my intellect would be belittled and challenged. I was not allowed to use slang or ebonics, but I had to always articulate with standard English.

What young child wanted to be a formal speaker 24/7 in all environments? Little did I realize that they were preparing me to evolve as an articulate young man who needed such competencies to survive in the future. In essence, I was introduced to the notion of why it was important to have a standard of excellence – to achieve and survive. The nuns at Saint Augustine's, were not naïve or oblivious to the life challenges that most of their students confronted on a regular basis, and they did their best to provide a safe zone for us. They also knew that it was difficult for young black males to accept them as role models. Quite simply, the nuns were up against the flair and dare of the brothers with 'street creds' that the young males admired.

My loving relationship with the nuns at St. Augustine influenced many of my future beliefs and decisions. For example, during the seventh year of residence in my Ph.D. program at Cornell University, I decided that I needed to seek a teaching position at another university or college. After all, my graduate stipend was barely enough to support myself, my young child, and my female partner. I applied to institutions in warmer climates and despite receiving offers from most of them, I accepted the offer from Xavier University of New Orleans – the only Black, Catholic University in North America, founded by Mother Katherine Drexel and the Sisters of the Blessed Sacrament.

I knew that would be a welcoming environment, and I could trust the nuns. The Oblate Sisters of Providence at St. Augustine's Elementary School, directly and indirectly, assumed the personal, moral, and spiritual responsibility that belonged to my absent parents. They were the angels on earth who understood and lived by these proverbs:

"For He shall give His angels charge over you. To keep you in all your ways." **Psalm 91:11**; and *"Even so it is not the will of your Father who is in heaven that one of these little ones should parish."* **Matthew 18:14**

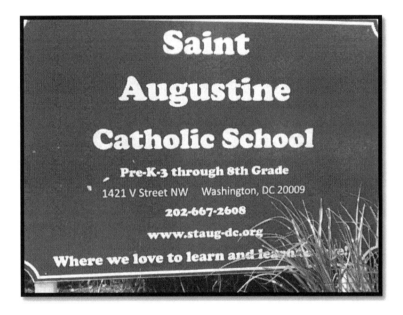

CHAPTER 5
THE LURE OF THE STREET

During any time of the year and in any kind of weather one could find me outside the apartment "hanging out." Mrs. Dawson and I would exchange a caring banter as I headed out of the apartment,

"I'm going out for a little while," I would say. "It's never for a little while, what time will you return?" she asked.

"When I come through that front door, it means I am right on time," I laughed. Her tone became very serious,

"Remember what I always tell you: Be careful, stay out of trouble's way because he is roaming the streets looking for you."

And then in a soft, caring way came a request, "If something happened to you, I don't know what I would do. I would be without my little man."

I knew she was sincere when she said this. She never went to bed until I came home, instead I would find her sleeping in a chair that faced the door. As I walked down the stairs, I thought "Mrs. Dawson has an older son and daughter, so why would she feel alone if something happened to me?" Anyway, I exited through the screen door out onto Corcoran Street: my playground, classroom, film studio, unexplored urban jungle, and training ground for the rites of passage. I first stopped at David's house to pick him up.

David and I were close friends, I guess because I was one of his protectors. He was physically challenged with cerebral palsy. His face lit up whenever he saw me, and his mother was so glad that I was David's friend.

She often said to me, "You make such a difference in his life, and I rely on you to get him home safe and sound."

I assured her that I would. The next stop was at Peach's house: a noisy place with a lot of kids and animals. I would never go in, I preferred to linger at the door. As the three of us walked up the street, we tried to develop our plan for the day but there was no consensus. Six and seven-year-old kids can get very excited in their decision-making, but the reality was we had limited funds. Days started this way until thru random conversation we stumbled upon some type of a plan, and sometimes it was uneventful but other times it seemed seismic to us. I seemed to be the only realist among our trio.

"Well, what are we going to do dudes?" said Peaches. We called him that because he loved eating peaches, sometimes five or six at a time.

"Man, the first thing we need to do is get some gapples, then we can do whatever we want," I stated confidently. I don't know why we called money gapples back then, but it sounded cool, so we went with it since we heard the older guys make that reference.

"I am going up to 14th and U streets where the street cars let-off and pick-up a lot of people, and beg for some money," I said.

"I have my lucky begging sign and collection can and I'm going to focus on women."

I had learned that women felt sorry for kids who beg, and they will give you money more than men. My sign was witty and emotional, and it read:

> *"No parents, No family.*
> *God will reward you.*
> *Thank you."*

As I walked away, I said, "You two decide what you are going to do, but let's meet back near my porch in two hours."

"Ok dude, look real poor and desperate and charm those women," Peaches said.

That was not hard to do. My sneakers were flapping because they were losing the tread, my jeans had holes and tears, and my t-shirt had been washed so much that it was hard to tell the original color. The only set of clothes that I kept decent was my Catholic school uniform. I took it off as soon as I returned to the apartment after school, so I was not tempted to play in my treasured outfit. It was one of the few material things that I really valued, owned, and cared about.

Begging And Survival

As I neared the green and gray streetcar stop, I headed toward a strategic spot where everyone walked by. As I predicted, the first coins to be dropped in the bucket came from several women.

One of them said to me, "Honey, please get your mother to buy you some KEDS (sneakers)."

She knew nothing about my life, but she had good intentions. A young couple approached me and the woman said to her male companion, "Dear, please give me a dollar to put in this cute little boy's can."

"Are you crazy," he responded.
"He is just a little hustler. Don't give him a damn thing because all they do is beg."

I thought: 'Just another jerk who did not care.' And so, they just walked on by. A Negro gentleman stepped off the streetcar. He was dressed so clean that he looked like he was a model in *Sepia* magazine which was founded in 1947 to highlight the achievements of Negro Americans. He dropped three one-dollar bills into my can, and I grinned from ear to ear, thanking him profusely.

He gave me his business card and then said: "You seem like an industrious young man who probably wants to earn some money. I have a lot of work over at my house and I would pay you twenty dollars if you come and help me. Let's go right now."

My radar immediately went up. The old heads in the Ledroit Park gang schooled us young boys, about slick men who wanted to get you into their house or apartment and rape you, tie you up, and kidnap you. I thanked him for the money and the business card and moved on to other targets. After 90 minutes, I had collected $8.35.

I headed back to the apartment to meet up with my boys. They had been busy too. They had broken into a few parked cars and stolen valuables. It is amazing that people leave valuable items visible in their car as if the world was honest and secure. We would take those items to the gang and they had connections to sell them, and they would slip us a few dollars for our work.

The three of us were starving so we visited our favorite deli and chowed down. We loved candy apples, milkshakes, and burgers. After finishing our meal, we started to walkback to my apartment. Nearing the building, we startled a skinny young boy who lived across the street from me. I had seen him occasionally, and each time he appeared to be a different kid to me. He dressed differently (sometimes in a cowboy outfit) and acted odd, but we knew that he was harmless, and he also had something that none of the other kids in the neighborhood possessed: TWO PARENTS. Every other kid had one or none. I don't think that I ever knew his real name.

"Hey dude what's up?"

"I'm playing cowboys and Indians, he said."

"Where are they, little man? I don't see either," I asked.

"They are in my imagination," he responded.

In retrospect, as I reflect on that conversation, I realize that at that age, I seldom imagined something that wasn't reality. I also never projected what was going to happen in my future. I was stuck at trying to survive, trying to connect the dots. A Negro boy becoming a cowboy was never going to happen!

Although the cowboy and I didn't have a relationship, little did he know that no other kids messed with him because he was protected by the Pee Wee echelon of the Ledroit Park gang. That was us: me, Peaches, David, and 4-5 other boys who fancied themselves to be in training. Why? Because the cowboy's mom was an angel. She knew most of us were dirt poor and did not eat regularly, so occasionally she would feed us baloney sandwiches, and this made us feel valued.

SIX DECADES later while living in Fayetteville, NC, a set of circumstances brought the cowboy and I together for the first time since our youth. I learned his name was Robert and he served as the Executive Director of the United Way organization, and now we are trusted friends. He also introduced me to his mother, who is 102 years old but as lovely and smart as ever. He arranged for me to eat lunch with them one day, and I teared up when I saw her and hugged her because she was a huge piece of the puzzle from my former life.

"Thank you for the sandwiches," I said.

But neither she nor Robert remembered giving us the baloney sandwiches. I remembered because when you are starving you distinctly remember anyone who cared enough to feed you: she was another woman and another angel in my life. I will never forget her and her son. I was blessed to meet them at that time in my youth, and more blessed to find them many decades later. Just as I protected him when we were kids, I will still protect Robert for the rest of my life. He has become somewhat cooler and is a true humanitarian.

As I noted, his mom is 102 years old, and I guess God allows some angels to spend more time on this earth until their work is done. I am jealous of the loving relationship that exists between the two of them, yet I love to be around both.

Robert Hines, Dr. Anderson, and Marie Hines (Robert's Mother)

It is quite strange how calm I feel around Robert today, and I attribute this to the safety net that he and his mother cast to the *'lost boys'* of Corcoran Street, NW (Washington, DC).

One of the treasures that he has retained is a black and white photo of him in his cowboy outfit, and I feel emotional each time I look at it. By chance, I found one of the only pictures that I possess of myself from when I was a young kid. I sent it to Robert recently and noted in an email:

"This is what your guardian angel/protector looked like as a young kid."

Marie Hines

Dr. James A. Anderson

Robert Hines (The Black Cowboy)

CHAPTER 6
MONEY EASILY BECOMES DANGER

Most young boys in the neighborhood competed to obtain any type of informal employment, and it didn't matter what it paid.

There were several older adults that relied on me, periodically, to run errands for them, but that was not predictable income. All of us kids knew of the one person who lived on the block, who frequently sat on his porch and called out to us to run errands.

We also understood that if you did go to the store or the sub-shop, upon return, you were ONLY to receive payment on his porch. Over and over, we had heard the admonishment:

"NEVER GO INTO HIS APARTMENT BECAUSE HE IS A PERVERT AND A PEDOPHILE AND YOU MAY NOT COME OUT UNSCATHED."

Most of us did not know his name but we created one for him – 'Fat-Nasty.' He was obese, dirty, and foul-mouthed, and he was known to try and entice young boys into his space by saying lurid and erotic things to us, and then he would attach the lure of money.

One day, I said to David and Peaches, "I need some money for groceries because at home our refrigerator is empty. I'm thinking about going to get some groceries for Fat-Nasty."

"Are you crazy?" they screamed.

"Alan, you know how sick and scary he is. Do you want us to go with you?"

"No fellas, I got this. I won't go inside."

Soon, I would come to regret those words. I met him on his porch and received a shopping list and some money. He smelled like a garbage dump and his teeth and gums were cruddy. I stressed to him that I would meet him on his porch upon my return.

I completed his shopping list in about 30 minutes and headed back to my block and his apartment, but when I arrived the porch was empty.

I walked over to the screen door and hollered inside, "I'm back with your groceries and your change," but I only heard the echo of my voice.

As I looked through the screen door, I could see the kitchen down a short hall. I thought that I can run in, set his groceries down and get my payment later that day. I carefully eased thru the screen door and walked quickly to his kitchen table.

As I set his groceries down, I heard the front door slam shut and the words, "Before you leave here you have to do something for me before you get paid."

I responded, "I want my money bitch, so pay me and I will leave."

"You are not going to leave until I get some ass from you," he said confidently.

At that point my heart sunk and for the first time I felt true terror. I didn't know exactly what he meant, but it didn't sound like he wanted to play checkers. I did sense that what he said involved sex, especially involuntary sex. I knew I could not run past him to exit the front door, hence I started to scan his apartment rapidly looking for a way out.

As he moved closer, I noticed that in the dining room was a large table and I immediately ran under it thinking that there was no way he could get his fat ass under this table. He was smart though because he kept pulling the chairs away from the table hoping to expose me and pull me out.

As I began to panic, I looked to my left and saw a large picture window. I gritted my teeth and surmised that a few cuts from broken glass would be more acceptable than to be captured by 'Fat Nasty.' I quickly moved from under the table, took two steps, and jumped through the glass. I assumed that the window was at street level and I was shocked as I jumped to sense that I was flying one level higher than I had expected.

As I crashed to the ground, I put my hands down to break my fall, but this resulted in two fractured wrists, a fractured ankle, and numerous cuts and bruises. I spent 4 days in the bed incapacitated. David and Peaches were at my bedside multiple hours each day, and I was reminded by them of the admonishment not to go into Fat Nasty's apartment:

"Man, we told you not to go into Fat Nasty's crib, you are damn lucky that you made it out," they said with slight derision.

I responded, "Look I don't need grief from you two. What I want you to do is to find some of the older gang members and let them know they have a devil on their turf (I was too young to know the word 'predator'). He cons young kids."

David didn't understand, "Why do that, what's is it goanna accomplish?"

"Look dude," I said, "I am sick of him scaring all the young kids on the block. He needs to be shot. None of us have a gun, so let's go to those who carry the heat."

Then I felt pangs of guilt from my Catholic upbringing.

I was speaking out of anger, "You guys know I don't really want him shot, don't you? The gang will figure out how to deal with him."

About three weeks later as I walked the block another neighborhood boy who we called 'Blue' came up to me and said, "Man, I don't know how you did it, but all the kids are happy that Fat Nasty is gone."

What? I had not heard this, but I felt vindicated. This time I went to get David and Peaches before I walked down to that viper's crib. Arriving there we were stunned. His apartment had been cleaned out and the neighbors told us that it was not by real movers. They said a few days ago, four men pulled up in front of Nasty's crib and then went inside. The neighbors said there was a lot of arguing and then Fat Nasty walked out with the men and got into the van.

He has not been seen since. The next day a small truck had arrived, and three men went into Fat Nasty's place and began to move things out. After they took what they wanted they told the neighbors that they could have anything that was left.

As we walked back up the street I said to David and Peaches, "Let's agree right now that when there are certain situations that could be potentially dangerous, we will always approach them together. No more Lone Ranger stuff like my dumb ass did."

As we walked up the street, I mused that it was now time to begin my training to join the Ledroit Park gang for protection. I knew that I was too young to engage in the real business of the gang, but the gang liked having a younger group that they could groom into the business.

I had approached several older members who I knew, and I asked them questions about gang-life. I would talk to them about escaping the clutches of 'Fat Nasty' type dudes and that I needed the protection of the gang. At first, they did not think that I was serious. They laughed and walked away.

CHAPTER 7
THE RITES OF PASSAGE (7-10 years old)

These were very significant years, and during this period I emerged as a man-child: sometimes by choice, sometimes out of necessity, and other times by chance.

These years would become the most traumatic period in my young life to date. I walked over to Ledroit Park to look for one of the gang leaders. About 20 members of the gang were there, and I asked if Yates, the leader, was around.

Their response was: "Little man what do you want?"

"I want to join the Ledroit Park gang." I said confidently.

"And what could you do for us, aren't you still sucking on your mama's tit?" They all snickered and laughed.

"I don't have a mother, never have." I said showing a little anger.

"Well, what skills do you bring that you feel can benefit this gang?"

I preceded to run down my brief resume of crime: breaking into cars, stealing food from the grocery store, begging for food and money, providing surveillance for the presence of other gangs on our turf and protecting weaker kids and older adults. I suggested that they could groom me to be whatever they needed.

"Come back this evening after we discuss you," they said

"Ok, I promise I'll return."

I was exhilarated, floating on a cloud as I walked back to Corcoran Street. When I returned to the apartment, I told Peggy about my visit to Ledroit Park.

"Alan, you need to leave those thugs alone. You are going to end up in jail or dead."

I chuckled and put my arm around her, "You know I would never leave you; I'm supposed to protect you." She shook her head and walked away.

Street gangs have historically received a negative connotation, and sometimes that reputation was well-deserved. I learned about violent gangs in other cities: in Chicago – the Blackstone Rangers and the Latin Kings, in New York – the Harlem Knights and the Jamaican Posse, and in Philadelphia – the 21st and Diamond Gang, the 12th and Oxford Gang, and the Italian gangs of south Philly.

The Ledroit Park gang valued territory and money, but, when necessary, they would lay the wood to anyone who challenged them. They were the largest gang in D.C., and they took the time to recruit and groom young street boys who would be mentored by older dudes. The gang had developed a set of protocols that *'prospects'* had to endure and overcome, but a better way of viewing them is to see them as *'rites of passage.'*

These are the processes by which young dudes are socialized in terms of feeling, thinking, believing, and behaving. Among the outcomes of this socialization were:
- how to live and survive in a difficult environment
- what it means to be a young Black man in a white world
- how to deal with females (young and older)
- ideas about sex, sexual relations, and wearing protection

- what is proper and improper behavior, and what is right and wrong
- protecting your gang, your family, and your hood (community)
- a loyalty to one's gang and no fear of other gangs
- how to earn and maintain respect
- the evolution of Negro/Black identity linked to manhood
- how to deal with the man (police)

One of the early tests imposed upon prospects was that one had to drink a shot of gin and then smoke some marijuana. My little eight-year-old body could barely tolerate this. I got sick like I had never been before, I laid on a park bench and slept soundly. When I awoke, I could barely stand up as I looked around, and nothing seemed familiar. I heard the laughter of the older gang members and one said, "Little man you passed the first test," and from that moment on, I never touched gin and reefer again, although occasionally I did sell weed for the gang.

To walk down a street in any major city and to be respected, is absolutely one of the best feelings. That is what I thought I wanted, but over time I learned that most of the world could care less about the Ledroit Park Gang. Over the next few months, I was assigned menial tasks by the gang: Go to the store and steal food, go break into some cars, go beg for some money (which I had to give to them), shine their shoes (they loved wearing Bally's, an expensive brand), etc.

Occasionally, the young boys in training had to fight one another and the older thugs would bet money on who would win. Sometimes you fought some kid who was 2 years older than you and 20 pounds heavier. The young Gladiators had to fight until blood was drawn, and I hated fighting for sport.

One evening, 'Smooth Eddie' told me to hang out with him. Eddie had stature in the gang because he was a major money earner and a ladies-man. Everyone knew that "Smooth Eddie" was the consummate pimp. He was always dressed sharp and possessed a smooth vocabulary that could melt the defenses of any woman. That is how he lured so many unsuspecting women into the business of prostitution. He never engaged in violence or fighting because he was too cool for that.

We walked to U street where the action was, especially with the ladies of the night, selling their bodies to any man with money. I was mesmerized because so much activity was occurring. Grown folks were laughing, arguing, selling, and buying drugs, parking fancy cars, preening like peacocks in razzle-dazzle outfits, playing the numbers, and sometimes a fight broke out, but order was quickly restored by members of the Ledroit Park gang.

"Little man, stay here while I go and talk to these hustling ladies," he ordered.

I knew he MEANT to stay where I was. I watched him glide past individuals and everyone showed him deference. He went to the area where a man in a car would stop, and one of the women would approach to chat with the driver. I saw Smooth Eddie talking to each lady, and then he would write something on a piece of paper. He walked back over to me and said:

"Take this list and this money and go down the street to the sandwich shop and purchase what's on the list. I must keep the ladies fed so they will have energy."

Innocently I asked, "Why do you feed these women, do you know them?"

He said, "Dumb ass, they work for me and the gang. I'm responsible for collecting money from them. I'm a pimp, do you know what that is?"

Quickly, I responded, "Not really, but I have heard that word used. Let me run and get the food before the shop closes." I started to run through traffic.

When I returned, he told me to take the food and drink over to the women. I did and as I gave them each their order, I received a tip. It was at that moment that I saw her, and she was as beautiful as an Egyptian Queen with those multi-colored cat eyes. Her name was Tina. Like the other women, she had to make a living, but she was so damn "fine." I asked myself why does she do this? Any man would be honored to call her his lady and support her. Over time, I became increasingly more comfortable being with them. Sometimes, they would even hug me and tell me that I would become a handsome pimp one day. Tina never said that to me.

Why would they say that to me, I thought. I had never stated that I aspired to that goal. What I later learned was that "Smooth Eddie" had mentioned to them that he was going to bring a young boy with him that he wanted to groom into the business, and they were to be nice to me. One of the older ladies named Rosebud, pulled me close to her one day and sternly said,

"Little man, do not get involved in this life because you will have to mistreat and brutalize women if we don't make your money right."

I became uncomfortable in response to her words, so as Smooth Eddie and I walked away from that area of action, I asked him two things:

"Man, why did those ladies say you were grooming me to be a pimp? Also, why did they seem afraid of pimps?"

He glared down at me,

"Shorty, everybody in the gang has a role to play. At the end of the day, it all about the gapples. We watch the young boys and identify where we think they will fit in. You are not one of these violent young thugs who fights all the time, rather you are calm, reserved, handsome, you speak well, and are smart, and we asked some of the boys at your school about you. Personally speaking, you could become as accomplished a pimp as I am."

I must admit that I felt charged about being compared to him, hence I decided to hang with him for a while. The strain of having so many different identities was starting to wear on me, especially among those areas that were in conflict. The nuns thought of me as a good Catholic boy. I was a street urchin who stole when necessary. I loved my sister and treated her with respect, but I was being groomed to be a pimp who often threatened and disrespected women. I protected my sister, David, and the cowboy but, I also sought the protection of the Ledroit Park gang. I could not shake the piercing death of Ms. Dawson, my beloved caretaker. I was now drowning in a cauldron of instability because I had no markers, no boundaries. I could come and go as I pleased, but I lost confidence in my decision-making.

Peggy must have told the nuns about my distress because one day I came home from school and there in the apartment sat two white people. I became very uneasy because I thought they were from an Agency who were going to take me, and possibly Peggy, away to place in a foster home. The woman spoke,

"I am Mildred, and this is Harry, my brother, we are Ms. Dawson's children, and I will be living with you two until we can decide what to do."

I was stunned. If they were Ms. Dawson's children, then they couldn't be white folk. Mildred did all the talking while

Harry just stood there looking cool. He was dressed in a tan suit with an exotic-looking tie, brown Bally shoes, and socks, and a cold-blooded gaberdine trench coat. He topped everything off with a sweet Dobbs gangster-brim hat and sunglasses. It was obvious that he was not going to take care of us. Mildred picked up her suitcase and walked back to the bedroom where Ms. Dawson used to stay. Harry said his goodbyes and eased out the door. Mildred came back into the kitchen, looked at Peggy and me and started to lay down some rules. I stood up and said,

"To hell with that, I don't know you and have seldom seen you before today. You and your rules can kiss my ass. You did not even tell us or the nuns that your mother had died."

I walked out of the room muttering to myself. I was angry, hurt, and confused and I began to think about how Mildred's presence would affect my life by placing limitations on my actions. I became very concerned with how Mildred would react when she learned that I was being introduced to the pimping business by the Ledroit Park Gang, and was seeking to be a member of the gang.

Smooth Eddie was looking out for me financially and professionally. For the first time in my life, I went grocery shopping and came back to the apartment with two full grocery bags. Mildred questioned where I got money to buy groceries.

I shrugged, and said, "Don't worry about it, it's all legal. I earned these gapples while working."

I noticed that Mildred carried a strange odor, and it was not because of poor hygiene. It was alcohol, specifically gin. I noticed on a regular basis empty gin bottles in the trash can, and sometimes she was so drunk that she would sleep an entire day.

The worst part of this scenario is that Mildred had a boyfriend named Francis, 15 years older than her, who was a wino, and he smelled worse than she did. He really had hygiene problems. I hated when he stayed over and slept in bed with Mildred. He developed the bad habit of eating anything and everything out of the refrigerator. When I asked for some grocery money, he broke bad with me and said that was my problem, not his. Remember, this is a grown-ass man talking to a young child!

I retorted angrily,

"Peggy and I can barely sleep because you snore like a bear, and when you are having sex, Mildred moans loudly and sometimes screams, and you often say crazy things." "The least you can do is give us some gapples to replace all the food that you have eaten."

After a couple of weeks, Mildred's presence was erratic–we would see her one week and then not for the next three weeks. During her absence, Peggy and I were alone, fending for ourselves. I preferred that because even when Mildred was there, she wasn't. She was either in a drunken fog or asleep. I also noticed that wino, Francis had begun to look at Peggy with predatory eyes. I asked her if she had sensed this, and she said she had, but she did not tell me because I might confront Mr. Wino and that would lead to serious conflict.

Mildred would probably support his denial and threaten that she was going to place us in foster care. That night as I accompanied Smooth Eddie to check on the prostitutes, I mentioned my dilemma to him. He said not to worry because he would have a talk with Francis. Eddie seemed to know who I was talking about, maybe it was because the Ledroit Park Gang sold drugs and alcohol to many addicted individuals. Whatever the case, I noted that wino Francis talked very little to Peggy and me for the next few weeks.

One afternoon, Smooth Eddie took me to a men's shop to buy me a new suit and some patent-leather shoes. I picked out the shirt, tie, and socks. He told me to wear it that night when we would go to collect money from the prostitutes. As we walked out of the store, I thanked him and asked him why he had purchased those things for me. He smiled and said, "Cause little man, you have graduated into the business, and you need to dress the part of an emerging pimp."

My heart almost stopped, and I did not know what to say. I was bursting with pride. He then turned serious,

"Alan, I need to tell you that when I am dealing with the prostitutes, whatever you see me do, it is always business. Never get emotional about business and never interfere with my fucking business. Is that clear?"

"Crystal clear," I nervously responded.

I would understand later why he was saying this.

CHAPTER 8
ADOPTED BY THE PROSTITUTES

I began to spend more and more time with the ladies of the night. After an exhausting night they would sleep until noon and wake up famished. Sometimes, they would send me to get them something to eat, and they would sit around the apartment and talk a lot of trash as they ate.

All conversations were reduced to a few topics: how men begged for sex and men's desire to have a "freaky bitch," or the ladies talked about which lady was dressed the sexiest the night before. As the banter sizzled, inevitably the older prostitutes would shout down the younger ones. One day, one of the younger ladies who called herself *"Cleopatra, the Queen of the Vile"* challenged Rosebud:

"You old hag, you have lost your beauty and your attractiveness to men. You need to go get a real job cause that's the only way you are going to make money."

Why did she say that? A fight ensued and it was the older women against some of the younger ones. Some of the younger ones did not like Cleopatra and they did not support her. The women cursed like sailors, threw food and clothing at each other, and questioned each other's ability to extract the most money from a "trick."

As this was occurring Tina, my favorite, would put her arms around me and say, "Don't be scared, they do this all the time, but they really do look out for each other."

We sat together on the couch while this mayhem continued, and Tina pulled me close to her to protect me. Sometimes they criticized Tina as being uppity because she was in medical or dental school (I can't remember which one). They were just jealous because she had beauty and brains.

It was not her fault that she had a greater financial need than some of these skuzzballs. She encouraged me to do well in school and not to become a pimp.

She used to say, "You are too sweet to go down that road of no return."

She did not have to worry because the nuns at St. Augustine's would kick my behind if I did not meet their standards of excellence. I would soon learn that the intimidation by the nuns was a reality.

The prostitutes would go to work about 9 p.m. and gather at two primary locations: 13th and U or 14th and U streets. Men would walk up to them and try to trade money for sex, but their preference was for men driving fine cars. Smooth Eddie would come to collect money from the ladies twice a night, first at midnight and then again about 3:30 a.m. He would confront each lady and ask how many tricks did they service that night, and what did the men want them to perform. He would calculate in his head what each woman owed. Everything was fine until he approached Tina.

"How many tricks did you pull tonight girlfriend," he demanded.

"Six," she said meekly.

"Bitch, don't lie to me. I know everything you women do every hour of the day."

Now, with fear in her voice Tina responded, "I have only serviced six men."

Eddie then turned and looked down at me and said, "Remember, anything you see me do is only business. No weak emotions are allowed."

Eddie began to pound the hell out of Tina while he said,

"Bitch don't ever hold out on me. You owe me money for eight tricks not six."

No other ladies came to her aid. So much for looking out for each other. Because Tina had protected me and looked out for some of my needs; I wanted to intercede and stop Smooth Eddie from assaulting her. Tears were streaming down my eyes as I watched the carnage and listened to Tina's screams. I shouted at Eddie,

"Leave her alone, she is begging you to stop." I prepared to attack him.

As he turned to address me, I could see on his face that he had gone to a different place. He was now evil, hateful, like a slave master terrorizing his slaves. He was giving the other ladies a lesson in what happens when you short the Pimp Master out of some of his money. As I leaned forward and prepared to jump on him, one of the other prostitutes put her arm down in front of me to stop my advance. She looked at me and said in a low voice:

"Do not mess with Eddie or you will end up like Tina, a bloody mess."

Eddie finally stood up and looked at the other ladies and said,

"I'll be back at 3:30 am and you better have my fucking money."

He slithered away like a snake.

Several of us rushed to help Tina up while the others went back to work hawking men in cars as they slowly drove by. My beautiful Egyptian Queen looked like a bloody, filthy rag that one sees in a dirty alley. She mournfully looked at me and asked,

"Can you walk with me back to the apartment, Alan?"

"Sure, come and lean on me as we walk," I responded quickly.

It was a struggle, but we made it back to the apartment. She asked me to run some bath water which I did. In a weak voice, she softly said,

"Help me to get undressed and then help me to get into the tub."

I did both in that order as I watched her sink her nude body into the hot water. I had never seen an adult woman without any clothes on. I was speechless and felt guilty that I had gazed on her bruised but beautiful body. I helped her into a nightgown and she crawled into bed. She requested a glass of ice water; I ran to get it. Before she fell asleep, she looked at me and whispered,

"My sweet little man I am so sorry that you had to see this ugly moment in the life of a prostitute. This is dangerous life for women. You saw that Eddie can be an animal. Baby boy, don't let that happen to you."

After seeing her nude, I also experienced my first erection in life. As she slept, I watched over her and I reflected on how much I had seen and experienced in my young life. I was proud that she trusted me, and I plotted about what I could do to retaliate against Eddie when I got older.

I also realized that if any man put his hands on my sister, Peggy, I would retaliate with a vengeance. Although I continued to be schooled by Eddie, I now despised him. He simply had become a ticket to cementing my status into the Ledroit Park Gang. One day, when I was older, I promised myself that he would pay for assaulting Tina. Up to that point in my life, I had never contemplated doing any action that was violent. I never was able to act on that fantasy because Eddie disappeared a few years after his assault on Tina. No one seemed to know what happened to him. I hoped his ass was dead.

CHAPTER 9
WHERE IS MY ACADEMY AWARD?

In the areas of D.C. where the prostitutes and pimps hung out, the owners of commercial establishments began to complain that their presence was harming their business and giving a bad reputation to the community.

The police began to cruise by more during the ladies' working hours in uniform and sometimes in plain clothes. It was difficult for the ladies to discern which normally dressed men were not plain clothed police. Increasingly, the ladies were getting arrested when they walked over to a car and solicited money for sex. The pimps were becoming anxious because they were losing money, and then they devised a new strategy.

Smooth Eddie told me to wear my suit, and patten-leather shoes that night. When I arrived, Eddie indicated that he and several other pimps wanted me to approach the cars initially, identify what the service men were interested in, indicate prices for different services, and then identify which prostitutes were best suited to do that.

At first, I could not understand why such a radical change was necessary. After all, I was only 9 years old and who would take me seriously. The ladies were experts at getting men to trade sex for money. I initially resisted this suggestion and began to walk away. Eddie stepped in front of me and said two hings that changed my mind: first, the police could not arrest a young kid of nine years, hence I was saving the ladies, especially my precious Tina, from getting arrested. It was the second point that both piqued my interest and initiated a flame of fear.

"Alan, we will give you $20 per night for putting in this work. You will become a legend. On the average, you will earn between $60 and $80 per week for a few nights work. We will start your training tonight, but if you refuse, you will not become a member of the Ledroit Park Gang, and who knows what will happen to you without our protection."

In either case, I was petrified. All the sudden the lure of money lost its luster because I was being threatened with exclusion. I must talk to Tina about this, but when I searched, I could not find her. I went through the first night of training unenthusiastically, but by the end of the week I had become an emerging actor. I learned to be careful with the words that I chose with the potential clients as they drove up. I was ready when the next dude drove up.

I announced, "My man, my man this is your lucky night. Do you see this bevy of beautiful ladies over there? One of them can be yours tonight for the right price."

One man angrily shouted, "Who the hell are you? Tell that hoe in the black miniskirt to come over here."

Confidently, I responded: "Sir, we must protect the ladies from getting arrested by the plain clothes cops. I can give you the prices for whatever sexual favor you want, tell you who is the best at satisfying your desires, and you can meet them at an apartment around the corner on T street."

I continued, "Our ladies have too much class to do sex stuff in the car with you."

After hearing the prices, the client indicated which lady he wanted, she would walk over to the car, and tell him where to meet her. I was now the bombastic showman of this sexual circus like P.T. Barnum.

"And the Oscar for illegal pimping, goes to the young man with the shiny suit."

Why such an elaborate deception? It was simple, the plain clothes cops would not arrest a woman until she discussed trading money (different prices) for sex. I would take care of this action, and even if the dude was a cop, he would not arrest a child. Despite my improvement, every night in my new role, I began to hate what I was doing.

It was not me, and it betrayed everything I had been taught by the Catholic nuns. Moreover, I had disappointed Tina who continued to counsel me about finding my future in school and not the streets. All this really came to a head two days later. Emotionally, it was exhausting work being a pimp, but my reputation and street credentials began to grow, and I was treated with a new kind of respect by my peers and even the old heads in the gang.

CHAPTER 10
THE NUNS TAKE CONTROL

I continued to attend school and do well. Monday morning was always "show and tell," when the students would briefly report what they had done over the weekend. To me, the other kids lived such dull lives, and their commentary reflected as much:

"I went to the zoo."

"I went to the mall with friends."

"I learned to swim."

"I went to the movies."

"I participated in a chess tournament."

When my turn came, I responded in a truthful manner, "I was working for the pimps and they were teaching me the business. The hardest part was memorizing the different prices for all the different sexual acts and…"

I was interrupted: "Stop, Stop, don't say another word Alan, I will talk to you after class," shouted the nun.
What followed was a low current of laughter and commentary amongst the other students. At the end of the school day, the homeroom nun escorted me to the principal's office.

Sister Consolata started in on me, "So, I understand that you are pursuing a career in a dirty, evil activity - PROSTITUTION! Is that right?"

"No, sister, I'm just trying to earn some money so Peggy and I can eat, and we can buy some cloths. We don't have any. Mrs. Dawson's daughter is never there."

"How did you get involved into this sinful behavior?" she asked.

"Sister, I was recruited to work by the Ledroit Park gang."

Sternly, she asked, "Where is the gang right now?"

"Probably out somewhere making money because they do whatever they want," I said.

"You may leave here now, but I want you to go find the gang leader and tell him I want to meet him tomorrow at 4:30 pm at the park." "Is that clear?" "You will go with me," Sister Consolata demanded.

As soon as I left her office, I ran to find Tina at the apartment where the prostitutes lived. Thank God she was there.

"Tina, I need some advice, please help me." Concern spread across her face,

"Come here and tell me what is going on. Do you want a sandwich or something to eat?" She could tell that I was upset.

I sat down and told her everything that happened that day starting with show and tell. But when I got to the part about the principal wanting to meet with the gang leader, she uttered

"Oh shit." She suggested that Smooth Eddie should also be part of the meeting.

Sheepishly I requested, "Can you come with me? I am nervous already. I don't know what Sister Consolata is going to say or do, and I trust you."

She said that would be fine.

The next afternoon Tina met me at school, and we walked to the convent to get Sister Consolata. As I introduced her to Tina, I said that Tina was in school and she looked out for me like a big sister. I was afraid to tell Sister Consolata that Tina is also a prostitute. Following a brief walk we entered the park. I could see Smooth Eddie in the distance, and standing with him was Yates, the gang leader. I don't remember much about Yates. He was a nice-looking dude, and because of his slight build, he probably could not rumble too well. What everyone knew was that he had spent time in Junior Village, the juvenile detention center, and in Lorton prison. Those experiences gave him automatic street creds. Sister Consolata addressed him,

"Mr. Yates, do you know what this young man said to the class two days ago. He said he was being trained to be a pimp by your gang. Is that true?"

"Yes sister," Yates stated, "We are preparing him to be part of the business, and the prostitutes really like him. Just ask Tina, she really cares for him."

Sister Consolata turned and looked at Tina and I with an angry look of betrayal.

She now knew that Tina was a prostitute. She continued to address Yates,

"Sir, I need you to free this little one from his gang responsibilities. He has a bright future ahead and he can escape this neighborhood and become something. Please do this, in the name of God."

Yates frowned at her and said, "With all due respect sister, God has nothing to do with running our business successfully. We link the right prospect with the right business and he will become a successful earner for us. Alan, is going to become a great pimp."

"Mr. Yates, I beseech you to help him," her voice increased in urgency. "He has no parents; no family and his life has been difficult. Please give him a chance."

This must have struck a chord with him. He looked Sister Consolata up and down and pronounced, "All right sister, this one time I will grant your request and we will let Alan go, but this is the last favor that we will grant. Don't think that the nun outfit you are wearing is going to soften my heart."

"Thank you, son, may God bless you," and she grabbed his hand within hers. I think that Yates gave her what she requested because he had been a student at St. Augustine's, and he still respected the nuns.

As the three of us walked back toward the convent, Sister Consolata quietly asked Tina, "Are you a prostitute working for the Ledroit Park gang?"

Her response was strong, "Yes sister, but I do it for a different reason than the other girls. I want to become a medical provider and help our community."

She then looked at me and continued, "When I learned about Alan's life situation, I decided I would be his protector. These are cruel, unforgiving streets sister."

As we neared the convent sister Consolata said, "Tina could you come in so we can chat for a while? Alan, you head on home." Tina hugged me and we parted company.

When I arrived at the apartment I sat on the stoop and tried to process the entire day. I was lost and confused. Perhaps if Sister Consolata had told me what was going to happen, I would have been more prepared for her confrontation with Yates. Where did this leave me now? I was no longer an emerging pimp and gang member. What was I? I guess just a little hustler who attended a Catholic school. I *thought: When the word got out at school and on the bloc that I was now estranged from the gang, how would I be perceived by my crew and others in general?* What now would be the source of my protection?

I began to worry about what Sister Consolata would say to Tina, after all they existed in different worlds. I was sure that their conversation would have ramifications for me.

A few days later, Tina was waiting for me after class and she said, "You did not tell me that you have an important program next week at your school."

I responded casually, "It's no big deal. I was not going anyway because I don't have any clothes to wear. It's some kind of spring religious festival."

Tina grabbed my hand, "Well, we are going to take care of that now. The nuns gave me some money to take you shopping. One of the prostitutes, Cassie, works downtown at Hecht's department store and she can get us a discount."

"Where did the nuns get money from? Didn't they and the priests take a vow of poverty?" I asked.

"Yes," she responded. "I think they do take such a vow, but they still get a small salary from the church. Most of their needs are taken care of so they can save their money."

We took the bus downtown and when we arrived at the department store, Cassie was waiting. She had already picked out a couple of outfits for me and wanted me to try them on to make sure the size was right. A few minutes later I emerged from the dressing room with a smile. I looked at them proudly and said, "They are a perfect fit."

They both hugged me and acted as if I were their son. Cassie bagged up the four outfits, and Tina and I headed back uptown. We stopped at the apartment first, and I tried on my outfits for the prostitutes who were there.

"Little man, you are too fine in those gray trousers, blue blazer, and blue Italian knit shirt," Rosebud said gleefully. I smiled and accepted her comments, after all, in their business they were experts in knowing how to praise a man.

We only stayed briefly, but when we left, I wasn't sure where we were going. So, I asked Tina and she replied that we were going to the convent. I nervously said to her, "Tina, the nuns now know that you are a lady of the night, I don't want them to give you a lecture about your choices in life."

"Alan, I talked to Sister Consolata and she assured me that would not happen. We have an understanding that we are joining forces for your well-being, hence we will limit our discussion about moral/immoral life choices."

I didn't believe that because the nuns seemed critical about everything. We arrived at the convent and were asked to come in. Three nuns were sitting on the couch, and two were standing. In front of them was a coffee table filled with cookies, chips, and punch. I began to drool since I had not eaten for hours. They provided a chair for Tina, who sat with them.

Tina then said to me, "Why don't you try on your different outfits for us." "There is a bathroom down the hall where you can undress." As I proceeded down the hall, I thought about how surreal all of this was. Nuns and prostitutes cared enough about me to pay for new clothes, so I could participate in a spring program. In a way, they were investing in me, and I could tell they cared deeply about me. I was humbled and I promised myself that I would never let them down.

As I modeled each outfit for them, they applauded me. Tina then said, "These are outfits for special occasions and are not to be worn when you are hanging out in the streets." Tina chatted with the nuns frequently and was treated like a special guest. Was it because of me? Had the nuns forgiven her for being a prostitute? I was never told why there appeared to be such mutual respect

I was no longer a pimp prospect, but I was still allowed to run errands for the ladies while they were working. I also took on a Robin Hood role for the kids on my block. Whenever they heard the ringing bell of the ice cream truck, they would run down the street after it, even though they had no money. For those who did have money, like the cowboy, the truck would stop and the driver would ask a kid what they wanted. He collected their money and then opened the door on the back of the truck, reached into the refrigerated section and pulled out the requested item. I watched this scenario intently and then devised a plan.

The next day, I hid between two cars and when the ice cream truck turned the corner, I jumped up on the back bumper, opened the door to the refrigerated section and started tossing out ice cream items to the kids running behind the truck. They were screaming with glee. As the truck neared the end of the block, I jumped off, but I was mad because I did not get anything for myself.

Duh! Duh!

I was a new champion for the kids on the block and planned to give a repeat performance. The next day, I listened for the ringing bell, and as the ice cream truck turned the corner, I again jumped on the back bumper, opened the door, and started throwing out ice cream items to the screaming kids running behind the truck. All the sudden, the driver slammed on the brakes, and my face and body slammed violently against the back of the truck. In a daze, I fell backward as my back and head slammed onto the ground. The driver emerged from the truck, stood over me and said, "Nigger that's what you deserve. Do you know how much money I lost yesterday because of you."

As my senses cleared, I noted that he was an older white man who was very angry. He opened the door to the refrigeration section, reached in, and pulled out an ice cream cone. Leaning over me, he rubbed it all over my face. As I tried to get up, he put his knee on my chest to hold me down, as he continued to rub this ice cream all over my face while laughing. Then he jumped back into his truck and drove away. This was my first negative direct encounter with a white man, and it was the precursor of more serious encounters with them that would follow in my life.

A second scary encounter with a white man occurred shortly after that incident. I became fascinated with trains and frequently went to Union Station to watch them leave and arrive. I often dreamed that I would ride a train to New York City. One day while there, I felt the urge to use the bathroom. As I approached, the public restroom, I noticed that a white man was standing at the long urinal relieving himself.

As I pulled down my zipper, he shouted at me: "Nigger, you are not supposed to be in here. The colored section is on the other side."

I didn't know what he meant but this crazy fool scared me. I quickly zipped up and ran outside. I guess I didn't see the sign that indicated, that 'White and Colored' represented different sides of restrooms. This was my first introduction to the politics of race and public accommodations.

Chapter 11
NEVER TO LATE FOR FORGIVENESS

The consistent absence of Mildred from the apartment put more pressure on Peggy and me to survive each day. Peggy continued to run errands for people, just as I did, and she also served as a babysitter periodically.

In addition, I added to my repertoire, stealing from grocery stores large and small, so, we could eat. I felt no guilt about larger stores , but I was always uncomfortable about the small mom and pop stores. There was one on my block and one around the corner, each ran by a very nice couple. The couple on my block understood the financial hardships of Negro customers, hence they allowed them to utilize individualized payment plans, and they also established personal relationships with them. I was too young to understand this then, but I now see, they were early practitioners of economic equality.

When she was alive, I would accompany Mrs. Dawson to that store, and I would observe how warmly the couple greeted us. There was a brief discussion of Mrs. Dawson's account, and she was told how much she could spend. Because of this relationship, I never stole from this store. However, the store around the corner became a regular target for me and my crew. We had grown expert, in terms of one of us utilizing distraction, to free the other two, to put things under our jacket.

David, Peaches, and I formulated our plan to be executed the next day: David walked into the store using his cerebral palsy crutches and fell out on the floor.

Peaches and I walked in about two minutes later, and we ignored David and headed for our targeted areas. Since we had no sense of nutrition, we wanted candy, popcorn, and peanut butter crackers affectionately called "nabs".

I loaded my pockets and suddenly I felt a hand grab my wrist, it was Mrs. Wilson. "What are you doing?" she shouted. "Are you three trying to steal from us after all we have done for the colored community."

My heart rate had now doubled, and I was way beyond thinking of this as a brief excursion by the three amigos. I kept trying to pull away, as her grip tightened.

David and Peaches had already run out and left me behind. Mrs. Wilson told her husband to hold me down while she called the police.

I began to picture a huge white policeman, with a night stick and a big death dog. In a moment of panic and before her husband had walked over, I tried once again to break free from her grip with no success—I then did the unthinkable and unforgivable – I reached up and gave her a mild slap in the face and she let me go. I ran out of the store still feeling a sense of terror but not relief.

So many thoughts were whizzing through my mind like a roller coaster. My behavior contradicted my fundamental values and sense of self. Had I become like Smooth Eddie by completely disrespecting women? Did I really hit a white woman – something Negro men got hung for down south? They were such a good couple, who helped the poor community, and now I had messed it up for everybody.

As always, when I was conflicted, I ran to find Tina. I had permission to just walk into the prostitutes' apartment, I did not have to knock, but sometimes I walked into a surprise. Most of the ladies were walking around in silk robes with nothing under the robe. Some were walking around with just a bra and panty set. Tina saw me and motioned for me to come sit next to her. She only had on a robe, and I averted my eyes while talking to her, nor would I look at any of the other scantily clad ladies. Tina noticed my sheepish behavior and said to the other ladies,

"You hoe's better put on some clothes because my little man is about to have a heart attack. And to think, Eddie wanted him to be a pimp." She laughed and continued, "He gets nervous just looking at a little skin." They laughed and she hugged me. I began to talk about the crazy scene in the Wilson's store. Tina's face reflected disappointment and puzzlement. "Well, what are you going to do?" she asked.

"I don't know, what should I do, I don't want to be arrested."

Tina got up and went to make a phone call. She came back and said, "I'm going to put some clothes on and after I'm dressed, you and I are going to take a walk, so stay here."

When she came back, we headed out. Tina looked like a star even when she dressed casually. Men of all ages, were constantly speaking to her as they walked, or they hollered at her from their car. I was so proud, that she would put her arm around me as we walked. After about 20 minutes, I realized that we were headed towards the convent. I almost froze and said to Tina, "Please don't tell the nuns what I did."

"Please Tina, please."

"Alan, this is a very serious matter. You got caught stealing and then you assaulted a senior citizen. Sister Consolata and I are going with you so you can apologize to Mr. and Mrs. Wilson and ask them to forgive you."

When we arrived at the convent, Sister Consolata was ready. She did not even speak to me, as we walked the four blocks to the store and walked inside, I could tell that Sister Consolata had already talked to the couple. I was so embarrassed; I could not even look at them.

Sister Consolata spoke first, "Mr. and Mrs. Wilson, all of us are deeply embarrassed by Alan's actions. Quite frankly, the children who attend Saint Augustine's are constantly taught to respect members of their community and to never lie, cheat, or steal. When we talked earlier, I shared the difficult circumstances that he and his sister have encountered in life, so I hope you can find it in your heart to forgive him."

The Wilson's looked at me and asked, "Well young man, what do you have to say for yourself?"

I lifted my gaze from the floor and in a soft pitiful voice responded, "I have embarrassed myself, my school, the nuns, and those who care about me like, Tina. I know this sounds like an excuse, but I just wanted something to eat. At the apartment, the refrigerator is always empty. Mrs. Wilson, I committed a mortal sin by striking you. God may never forgive me. I am going to confession tomorrow, and reveal my actions to the priest."

Suddenly, Tina spoke up, "Maybe Alan, you might want to work for free at the store doing whatever the Wilson's need."

Mrs. Wilson looked at Tina, "What is your relationship to this little thief?"

Calmly Tina responded, "I act like his big sister and keep my eye on him. You can be sure, that I and the nuns at St. Augustine will increase our attention to his behavior, we promise you."

You could tell that Mrs. Wilson was doubtful, "Young man I can forgive the stealing, but hitting me in the face is unforgivable."

All I could think to say was, "Please give me a chance and have faith in me. I promise I will never do such ugly things either at this store or anywhere." Later when I thought about this last comment, I thought the Wilson's and the nuns would never forgive me.

Sister Consolata ended the conversation, "He will be here at the store at 3:30 p.m. after school every day for the next month," and Mr. and Mrs. Wilson nodded in agreement.

As the three of us walked back towards the convent, no one spoke. I was so upset that I had disappointed Tina and Sister Consolata. As we arrived at the convent, Sister Consolata just walked in without a word.

Tina said, "I hope you understand how serious this was. You could have ended up in Junior Village with all the other delinquents and young thugs."

I loved Tina but I wanted to say to her, "I feel bad enough so don't keep piling dirt on me," but of course she was my Cleopatra. That evening, back at the apartment, I told Peggy what had happened. Instead of dumping on me, she put her arms around me and held me close to reassure me. My angel understood that my unforgivable actions were to take care of her more than anything else.

My crew, David, Peaches, and I, decided we would engage in one of our favorite pass times: we would go down to the Washington monument and try once again to run up the stairs from the ground floor to the top. This was our fifth attempt at this unrealistic goal. You see, our little legs were too short, and we barely made it halfway up. To complicate this endeavor even more, we had to avoid the people who were walking down. So, we came up with the idea to holler a warning to anyone as we ran upward.

It was corny, but we liked it: "Watch out here comes the Monument Monsters." By the time we walked down, after another futile attempt, the white folk had complained to the gatekeepers who chastised us for scaring people. Whatever, it was fun!

At night, I went up to 14th and U streets to make some money by running errands for the ladies of the night. It was Saturday night and U-street was bustling, just like the pictures I had seen of the Harlem Renaissance. I saw Tina and I ran over to her.

She looked right through me and said, "One of the nuns called me and said that you had not turned in your math homework for two weeks. What's up with that?"

I was looking around at all the action and not really paying attention to her. In one swift motion, she grabbed my shirt collar, and escorted me over to a card table that sat under a streetlamp. I was told to sit down. the table was a legal pad, pencil, and copies of the homework assignments for the last two weeks.

She said, "I promised your math teacher that you would complete your homework, don't make me a liar."

So, there I sat, at 1:00 a.m. under a lamp doing math homework, while the world of excitement hummed all around me. I vowed to never find myself in this situation again. Some people walked by and laughed at me,

"What are you doing little man. Who the hell does schoolwork in the streets at 1 a.m."

I felt embarrassed and humiliated, but I didn't want to let down Tina and the nuns.

Chapter 12
THE SPELLING BEE
A Lesson in Humility

Over time I understood why it was important to perform well in school. I began to compete for various awards. Every fall there was a city-wide spelling bee competition for the catholic elementary schools. At St. Augustine's, the nuns held a competition to see who would represent our school, and I won.

On the day of the event, the students from different schools, were packed on a stage at an area high school, each with a large number on a sheet of paper attached to their clothes. The other students were identifying their parents and family members in the audience, by waving to them. There I sat alone as usual, with no one to wave to, no parents, no relatives, no loved ones. I became disillusioned and started to lose interest in this spelling bee. Suddenly, I heard my name called out in the distance. I scanned the crowd and about 15 rows back, in the center, I saw them.

There sat three nuns, Tina, and one other prostitute, and they had come to cheer me on. I perked up and stood up and waved at them. I was ready to slay my competitors. I breezed through the first two rounds. In the third round, I stood at the microphone waiting for my new word and heard these words from the judge:

"Please spell the word UNUSUALLY."

That was such an easy word, not even challenging, I thought. With supreme confidence, I quickly gave my response, and then I heard a dreaded sound, a sound that one associates with failure. It was a buzzer that indicated I had spelled the word wrong. I was stunned and in total disbelief. I saw the look of disappointment on the faces of my support group in the audience. When the program was over, they tried to console me. They all said the same thing, I tried to spell the word too fast. For the rest of my life, I have never forgotten the word "unusually."

In retrospect, that humbling experience was good for me. For the first time in my young life, I experienced anxiety while presenting in front of an audience. I was also anxious about competing against predominantly white contestants. Little did I know, that for the rest of my young life and beyond, I would be contending with white folk in school and in other professional pursuits. Generally, I had little to no support at these times and I bear the painful memories and emotional scars of these episodes. I must have been blessed with a deep reservoir of emotional strength, and self-belief to carry me through the times I considered giving up.

It was now the period between fall and the start of winter, and I began to worry about the onset of winter. Since Mrs. Dawson's daughter, Mildred, had all but abandoned us, I constantly thought about who would pay the rent and put food in the refrigerator. I knew one thing – I was going nowhere near the Wilson's store!

One day, David's mother, asked me if Peggy and I wanted to ride with them down to some city in Virginia to visit their family. I agreed for two reasons: first, I had never been to Virginia, in fact, I had never left Washington, D.C. second, I appreciated that David's mom thought to ask us, so how could I turn her down.

Once there, we met David's family members, and you could see the resemblance among all of them. Three of David's cousins were very fair, in terms of skin color, and were around our age. They suggested that we go outside and walk the neighborhood. As we walked, we encountered some of the cousin's friends. It was like meeting the United Nations, because of the racial diversity of the kids we met, but they all were friendly, that is, until we were approached by three White males.

One of the cousins spoke cautiously with a serious tone, "Here comes BB with two of his friends."

I asked, "What does BB stand for?"

The response, "Bobby Blade, because he always carries a knife."

BB and his friends seemed a little older than us. As they reached us, BB asked David's cousins who we (Peggy and I were. When he heard that I was from D.C., he looked at me in a condescending manner and said,

"Oh, you think you are one of those slick-ass Negro gangsters from the Big City."

My response was quick and confident, "First of all, I am not a gangster and yes, I am from a big city. At least I am not some country turkey like you and your boys."

Suddenly, everything got quiet, and the silence was that of an impending doom for someone. I knew David had my back, but he had cerebral palsy, so he was limited in his contribution to any rumbling. BB walked behind us as his two partners moved toward me. I kept my eyes on them and suddenly, I felt a knife against my throat; I knew it was BB behind me.

He now started talking smack to me, "Hey big city man, what the hell are you going to do now? If you say the wrong thing, I will slit your throat, Ni***r."

Peggy and two of the female cousins screamed, "Leave him alone, he didn't do anything to you."

I now realized the potential danger of this situation.

At that moment an older gentleman stepped out of the doorway of the house we were in front of, "I've been watching you troublemakers through my window, and I called the police," he said.

BB's partners immediately said to him, "Come on man, we can't afford to get caught with this knife."

Before BB pulled away from me, he whispered in my ear, "Nigger don't ever let me catch you in my city again." "Here is something to remember me by."

As he pulled away, he cut my neck slightly with the knife. Then the three of them ran down the street.

I was too angry to be scared, but this was my third negative encounter with a white male in just a few months (remember the ice cream truck driver and the train station). The seeds of anger and distrust were now planted.

When we returned to D.C., I went to visit the Ledroit Park gang, and I requested they avenge my treatment by BB and his crew in Virginia.

Yates responded, "You are not a member of the gang, and you are no longer in training. So, you are on your own. If you were in the gang, we would drive down to Virginia, and lay the thunder down on BB and those punks."

I knew it was a waste of time to argue with them. Not too far away, I saw Smooth Eddie and thought maybe he would avenge me. I described to him what happened, he mockingly laughed and said:

"Little man, as you know I am a businessman, and I don't have the time to deal with your grade-school bullshit. I understand that you are angry with this white dude, but you must learn how to handle your own business."

I started my walk home and sucked-up my frustration. I should have been thinking about how close I had been to getting my throat cut.

Chapter 13
THE DISCONTENT OF HOLIDAYS AND THE WINTER

Whenever a holiday was approaching the nuns at St. Augustine would have the students create artwork about that holiday. In one of my classes, the students were given a Thanksgiving card with a picture on the front. The students had to recreate this into a drawn picture they would color.

I was given a card that was difficult to draw and color: a dining room in a home that was full of food on the table including a huge cooked turkey. I did my best, but it was so challenging. The nun collected all the pictures, hung them around the classroom and invited other nuns to review then after school.

One afternoon, I had to stay after school for detention, and I was sitting there by myself. I can't remember what I had done, but it did not matter because the nuns were the authority and whatever they said was law. Two nuns came into the classroom to look at the pictures.

One stood in front of my picture and said, "This is very good, look at the attention to detail."

"Sister, which one of your students did this one?"
She pointed to me and said, "If this one could only stay out of trouble."

I thought to myself: What did she mean? I am seldom in trouble at school. At most, I would get placed in detention usually because of talking in class. The nuns did not have an inkling that major holidays had little meaning for me. I had never experienced '*Thanksgiving*' as most people know it. How could I? When Mrs. Dawson was alive, she could not afford to purchase a big spread of food. Moreover, with no family in my life, what did I have to be thankful for. The scenario that I just described also held true for Christmas. I never had presents nor a Christmas tree. About the only happy thing that happened was that Peggy, David, Peaches, and me would go downtown and look at all the Christmas lights in department stores. I was not the only kid in D.C., who lived through such a holiday vacuum. I am not sure what the lasting emotional effect has been, of being deprived of the joy of such celebrations. I do know that I had few actual expectations that preceded holidays. Why would I?

The absence of expectations did not mean that I did not have wishes and desires. I fantasized about having a family, celebrating an authentic Thanksgiving and Christmas.

I can remember Tina taking Peggy and me downtown to a department store to see Santa Claus, and as we waited in line, she said to us, "Now think about what you are going to tell Santa what you want for Christmas."

When my turn came, at first, I was afraid to sit in this white man's lap, but I finally did. When he asked what I wanted for Xmas, I was as honest as I could be,

"Man, I want a mother and father for me and my sister, I want some food for the refrigerator, I want a warm winter coat since I'm always cold, and I want some money for Tina because she needs to finish school without having to be a hoe."

Santa was speechless at first, but then he said, "When you say your prayers tonight before going to bed, ask God for those things because none of that stuff is in Santa's gift sack."

I jumped off his lap, turned and looked at him and said, "I knew you was a fake, fatso."

As the weeks passed the apartment grew colder because there was no one to pay the bills, and then my greatest fear was realized. One evening, this old white man came to the apartment and told Peggy and me that we would have to leave, because the rent had not been paid in months. I told him that Mildred was there sometimes, but it didn't matter because she was not paying the rent anyway. He did not know Mrs. Dawson had died.

For the next few weeks, Peggy and I lived in the street and that experience made us feel less valued than the rats that ran freely. At the corner of 14th and R streets was a tire store, and sometimes we would sleep inside a row or tires that sat elevated on a rack. Before we entered the tires, I would take a can of Right Guard deodorant and a cigarette lighter and spray the–deodorant across the flame thus creating a mini-flame thrower. That was to drive out any mice or rats hiding there. I had to sleep with one eye open in case any rodents returned.

When it snowed and became colder, I started breaking into cars in near-by parking lots. We would sleep awhile and rise early before the lot opened for business.

If that alternative was unavailable, we would find a large grating on the sidewalk, where steam rose from underground, and about 4 or 5 other kids who were homeless, would huddle together under blankets to sleep. We alternated which child would stay awake for 2 to 3 hours, to watch for stray dogs and sexual predators. Whenever one or more white policemen walked by and looked at us, they would just laugh and keep walking. I always wondered if they were black cops, would they do the same thing, but I had never seen one and I doubted if they existed. White authorities didn't care about poor, abandoned black kids.

Our favorite grating was at 14th and S street next to the telephone company building. In the morning, when people were entering the building, they would see us sleeping on the grating and offer us a few dollars to get some breakfast. Most of them were white women and I began to think that some white folks were okay.

Every now and then, we would have a heavy snow in D.C. and the gratings just were not going to get it. So, I was back to breaking into cars, so we could sleep there. After several days of this lifestyle, all the kids smelled like funk balls because we had not had a bath. Once again, creativity saved the day. We would go to one of the area gasoline stations and wash up until some employee ran us off.

During the winter, the ladies of the night were still on the corner doing business. It seemed they were wearing the same type of clothes as in the summer. How did they do it because it was freezing? Over time, new prostitutes would join the group and others would leave. The older group was either not earning enough or received complaints from some of their customers. I am forever grateful for the attention, care, and constructive criticism that I received from them. I can say the same thing about the catholic nuns at St. Augustine's Elementary School. They drove me hard, challenged me, and supported my self-confidence. In their own way, they were preparing me for manhood while supporting my self-confidence. To this day, I still can't believe that they joined forces to help me (and Peggy) to survive. I won the lottery in heaven and was sent angels.

It was not until I got older, that I began to realize that I was depressed during much of my childhood, and this carried over until my adult years. Every young child has experiences that are positive and negative, but continuous traumatic events can lead to serious emotional outcomes that have longevity.

Up to the age of 10 years old, so much of my life was about basic survival devoid of emotional anchors, especially a mother.

I had struggled because I had longed for a mother to hold me, to tell me she loves me, to be there when I was afraid or felt insecure, and to apologize for my abandonment. Mrs. Dawson gave me a chance when she brought me home from the hospital, and in her own way she showed warmth and caring. Maybe she did not invest more, because she knew I could be taken away at any time, or maybe the simple fact was that I was not her child, but her sacrifice was a miracle. I have maintained one consistent memory of her, that is, I see us sitting at a table in the kitchen and she is helping me with my homework.

Every now and then, she would run her fingers through my curly hair and remind me that God would take care of Peggy and me when she died. I would get nervous whenever she said this, because it sounded like she knew that this prediction would soon happen.

Dr. James A. Anderson

Chapter 14
A Forced Leap into The Unknown

My life as a young boy was unpredictable to say the least, but what happened in a single day would place my life on a different course. I became perplexed about who I was, who I would become, and who was controlling my existence. My catholic training led me to believe that God or the angels and saints, were guiding me toward a fulfilling life, but the events that I am about to describe, caused me to lose my faith in everything- including myself.

Peggy and I had just finished our first few weeks back in our original apartment, I guess the nuns or the prostitutes, or both, found a way to secure our living arrangements. When Mrs. Dawson was alive, she seldom had visitors, hence I did not know any of her friends. One day, there was a knock on the door, and I answered. Standing there was an older woman, who I vaguely remembered, from her visits to Mrs. Dawson.

She smiled and said, "I am your Aunt Evelyn, and I was a very close friend with Mrs. Dawson. I am so sorry that she passed away. Do you two need anything because I am more than willing to get it for you."

"No thank you," I replied. She did not sit down, and she looked a little nervous.

"What have you both been doing since Mrs. Dawson died." she asked.

"We have been trying to survive, some days are better than others." I responded. I thought that this is such a dumb-ass question, and then she looked at me in a very uncomfortable way and said, "Alan, why don't you and I go for a ride so we can talk."

"What are we going to talk about, I seldom see you and I don't know you that well. I would rather stay here with Peggy," I said.

Aunt Evelyn seemed to get a little agitated at my refusal to follow her suggestion.

She then moved to a different strategy, "Alan, why don't you ride with me to the store, and while there you can pick out some dessert for you and your sister."

Now you have my interest, lady. I responded, "Ok, I can live with that. Peggy, what do you want from the store?"

Peggy was always two notches ahead of me, "So Aunt Evelyn, why don't you just give Alan some money and me and him can get the desserts. There is a good dessert place on U street."

Peggy had reservations about this woman and me going with her.

I could see that she was trying to help me, so I would not leave with this woman, but I finally relented.

"All right, let's go ma'am so I can come back and do my homework."

Peggy chimed in, "Yeah, I will stay here and do my homework."

 I put on my jacket and headed toward the door. I stopped in the doorway and turned and said to Peggy, "I will see you when I get back, I love you."

She responded, "I love you too, hurry back." Then she blew me a kiss. My angel loved and protected me, always.

That was the LAST TIME we would ever see each other. Not only was I unaware of my last name, but I also did not know Peggy's. Thus, my attempts to locate her have not been successful. That has become the gaping hole in my life, the source of unending sadness, and the reason why I lost my faith in people.

During the ride, Aunt Evelyn kept utilizing small talk, but it seemed as if she was just trying to distract me. We were riding through a section of D.C. I had never seen before. Streets were clean, houses were nice, and kids left their bicycles, unchained, laying on lawns or front steps. Shoot, David, Peaches, and me would have had three bikes each, at least. In the area of DC where I lived, if your car or bike was unlocked or available, within 15 minutes it would be gone.

Finally, I said to Aunt Evelyn, "We have been riding for a while, and if we had gone to the dessert store near the apartment, we would be home finishing our dessert right now."

She did not respond immediately but when she did, she suggested, "I just wanted to take you to a new dessert store." At a visceral level, I did not believe her because of the distance we had covered.

Finally, we parked in front of a lovely house and quickly I said with urgency, "Why are we stopping here, this is not a dessert store."

She then stated what would soon become an untruth, "I must speak to someone that I know for a few minutes about some business issues, so why don't you come in with me." I refused at first because I was uneasy but as she continued to ask me, I yielded. As we walked into the foyer, I could see into both the living room and the dining room. Wow, wow, wow! So clean, so nice, such amazing furniture.

Those two rooms were larger than our whole apartment. What really caught my eye was the real fireplace in the living room. I commented on it, and I was told there was also one in the basement. The older couple who stood in front of us kept staring at me as they talked to Aunt Evelyn who suggested that I wait for her in the den and watch television.

The three of them sat in the living room and talked for about 20 minutes. I saw Aunt Evelyn stand up and, I assumed we were leaving, so I walked towards her and stood near the door.

As she began to exit, she looked at me and said words that I will never forget: "Alan, you are not going with me now. You can stay here for a while."

Anxiously I responded, "When are you coming back to get me? We must get the dessert to take to Peggy." I was now extremely nervous.

She looked at me solemnly and said, "I am not coming back for you. *THIS IS WHERE YOU ARE GOING TO LIVE FROM NOW ON.*"

Even though she spoke these words with clarity, my psyche would not allow me to process them. Through the venetian blinds on the front door, I watched Aunt Evelyn get into her car and drive away. I was frozen in time and even though the older couple standing behind me tried to utter comforting words, I could not hear them. I refused to hear them. There were no words in existence that could have comforted me at that moment. I was still in disbelief that this was happening, I turned to this Black couple and calmly asked,

"When is she coming back to get me, and if she doesn't, then you need to drive me home."

"Son, we can't do that because it was not part of the agreement. We are going to do our best to give you a good home, a Christian home. Please try to understand."

"Part of "an agreement"? What damn agreement," I said angrily. My life and my existence had now been reduced to some "agreement." I did not agree to anything, so I guess my feelings didn't really matter. I was being moved around like a piece on the chess board, and I was angry beyond belief, and had a deep, deep level of sadness. I addressed the couple again and this time my anger and fury tinged every word I spoke,

"I don't know you two and don't care to know you. I need to be taken back to my sister right now, right now."

The woman put her hand on my shoulder and said, "This will be a better life for you, son."

Accounting for their age, I said respectfully, "Ma'am, is this dude your husband?" She indicated he was. I continued,

"I don't know where I am, nor who you two are. Nothing was explained to me. I am lost without Peggy, Tina, and the nuns."

Aunt Evelyn's visit to the apartment was a sham; she lied to Peggy and me. "What is going to happen to Peggy?" I asked sternly. I assumed that she was part of this equation.

They both responded that they didn't know, but they thought she was going to live with someone else.

"Alan, would you like something to eat?" they asked.

Although I was starving, I refused to accept their hospitality.

"The three of you kidnapped me and took me from the only person I love and trust. I don't know what is happening to her or where she will end up. All I can say to you two is that nothing negative better happen to her or I will burn this house down."

They told me that their names were William and Avor Anderson. Mrs. Anderson suggested that we go upstairs so that they both could show me my bedroom.

As we ascended, I commented, "You have the same rug on the stair steps as you do on the first floor."

I never knew that was possible.

As I walked into the bedroom, there was a nice bed, a dresser, a small table with a lamp on it, and a cross hung over the bed. On the bed was something wrapped in plastic. I asked what it was. I was told that they were new pajamas for a young man. I had never worn pajamas in my life. I always slept in a t-shirt and my underwear.

Night had fallen, so they suggested that I get ready for bed. I had my own bathroom full of towels, face cloths, and a bathtub. There was a shower, and my eyes lit up because I had never taken a shower, but my eyes were also full of tears. The events of the day had broken my spirit; I felt alone and abandoned. I promised that I would never trust anyone again. I did not sleep in the prone position as I normally do, but instead I pulled the light blanket off the bed and sat in the corner where the wall meets the bed. I pulled the blanket over my head to shut out this new, forced reality that was imposed on me. My last thoughts before I dozed off were:

"When they take me to school on Monday, the nuns at St. Augustine will get all of this craziness straight, and I will never have to come back here again."

For the rest of my life, I have called the events of that Friday: *"The Snatch in the Night."* I cried through most of the night. My life was shattered, I was terrified and in disbelief that no one told me that this was going to happen. Why did God let this happen to me? What had I done to deserve this horrific treatment? Was this happening because I had slapped Mrs. Wilson, or hung out with the prostitutes and the Ledroit Park gang? How can I contact the nuns, Tina, David, and Peaches? I was heartbroken and confused – abandoned once again.

CHAPTER 15
EXPLORING A NEW WORLD

When I awoke the next morning, the house was quiet, and I realized that I was alone. I saw a nearby clock and realized that I had slept about 10 hours. I guess that I was physically and emotionally drained from the events upheaval of the day before.

Moreover, the sadness and dejection had not dissipated. I walked through the four bedrooms upstairs and then went downstairs to the kitchen. I opened the refrigerator and then closed it quickly.

I opened it again slowly. I was surprised no stunned, at the amount of food that I saw. I had never seen a packed refrigerator. I did not recognize most of the items that I was viewing. I remember picking up a plastic cannister that contained "cottage cheese." I thought it would taste like the cheese you put on a hamburger. I stuck my finger into it to taste it and then spit it out on the floor. It was sour and nasty, and the texture was a taste that I could not compare to any food I was familiar with. Next, I saw a bottle labeled 'Prune Juice,' which I was also unfamiliar with, but I decided to take a swig and almost choked.

This taste-testing continued for twenty minutes. It wasn't until I tasted the banana cream pie that I smiled. I then realized that the Andersons had gone to work.

Suddenly, I thought why I am fooling around with this food, when I should be trying to escape. I ran to the front door and unlocked the bottom lock, but the top lock had a dead bolt lock. I did not have a key. This was true for all the doors on the first floor. Next, I thought to open a window and climb out, but as I started to lift it, I saw the decal for the alarm system on the glass pane. I realized an alarm would go off. I ran downstairs to the basement and experienced the same frustrations with the doors down there. So, I just sat on the sofa in the den, watched TV and waited for them to come back to the house.

When they did return, I asked if I could walk around the neighborhood to just explore my new environment. They denied my request. I know it was because they thought that I would run away. Damn skippy, I would be in the wind trying to figure out how to go back to my apartment. During mealtimes, I would eat nothing or very little, but instead, I would just look at Mr. and Mrs. Anderson and say, "Where is my sister? Take me back to her."

Their response was always the same, "We don't know, nor do we have any idea who would know." We wish you would focus on making a new life for yourself here in our home."

Quickly I would respond, "This is not my home and never will be. You seem like nice people, but I don't know you and don't want to live with you. Is that too damn hard for you to understand? When I go back to school on Monday, the nuns will address this fantasy of yours."

They didn't respond, but it seemed like I hurt Mrs. Anderson's feelings. I didn't care; I was the one kidnapped. The rest of the weekend was dominated by my silence and disinterest in anything that Mr. and Mrs. tried to talk to me about.

I can only reflect now on my inner reality during that crucial period. I am almost sure that I felt no sense of hope or curiosity about my future because I was mired in anger and confusion.

Even when Mr. and Mrs. Anderson repeatedly mentioned that I would have a better life, I refused to hear or believe them. In retrospect, they tried their best to give me hope and at the same time mollify my pain. I cried every day for months, and my prayers to God and the Virgin Mary went unanswered. Had the nuns and priests lied to me about the power of prayer?

CHAPTER 16
CROSSING THE RACIAL BOUNDARY

Monday morning arrived. I was excited about going back to Saint Augustine, so the nuns could free me from this temporary prison. After a short drive, we pulled into a large parking area, that sat in front of what looked like a Catholic school. I figured this out because the school sat next to a Catholic Church.

Mrs. Anderson turned to me and said, "This is your new school, Nativity Catholic School, and we will be back to pick you up at 4 p.m."

Defiantly I responded, "This is not my school. Take me to St. Augustine's, now." Calmly, Mrs. Anderson tried to encourage me, "Alan, you will enjoy this new Catholic School. We have talked to the nuns, they understand your situation and they will help you with your adjustment here, so try to make the best of it."

I exited the car and watched the kidnappers drive away. I turned around and looked at the students who were lined up by grade level, I guess. Once again, I was so confused and hurt. How many times was I going to be surprised with changes in my life? No one bothers to talk to me and explain why I am being moved around like a piece on a checkerboard.

Suddenly, I heard a voice, "Young man, why aren't you lined up with your class, what grade are you in?"

I turned around and stared at this white nun who was glaring at me.

I responded angrily, "Sister, whatever your name is, I don't intend to go to this school. I am walking over to that big street over there (Georgia Ave.) to catch a bus and try to figure out how to get home."

"No, you are not," she said sternly. You are going to line up with the other students."

Defiantly, I responded, "Sister, I respect you because you are a nun, but there's nothing but white kids over there and I don't want to go to school with them."

As the argument intensified, another younger nun walked over and said, "Sister Euthalia, this is the little one we talked about at dinner last night."

I looked at Sister Euthalia and smugly said, "Yeah Sister, I must be the one that you all talked about because I am the only brown spot on this playground."

The younger nun, Sister Regina, put her arm around my shoulder and escorted me over to the appropriate line. While standing there waiting to go inside, I heard 'it' for the first time from a kid in line behind me,

"Is this spook in our class now?"

That soon became a periodic sound bite that I became sick of. Three days later, while in a class, I asked the nun if I could go to the restroom. She said yes and to hurry back. As I walked down the hall, suddenly I ran towards the stairs, rushed down, and was outside the school. I ran over to Georgia Avenue; I kept running for two blocks and then waited at a bus stop. I had lunch money that I used when the bus stopped to pick me up. I just sat there as the bus passed block after block which was unfamiliar to me. Finally, after about 30 minutes, I realized that I was in downtown D.C. I got off that bus and started walking uptown. I generally knew how to get back to the apartment.

It was a long walk, but when I arrived, I ran upstairs and tried to open the door with the key that I had kept, and it worked. I walked in, not expecting to see Peggy, because she was in school, but my heart sank when I saw that the apartment was completely empty; I mean, nothing was in there. As I walked outside, two police officers were waiting for me. They had been sent by the nuns from Nativity School, who figured I would try to come to the apartment. I was taken back to Nativity School and scolded for running away.

I was also told that they had called Mr. and Mrs. Anderson, so I knew that I would get grief from them this evening, and I did, but I could care less. All of them could kiss my behind.

After four months, I accepted my fate. Some things in my life had improved: I had three meals a day, I had my own room, and I lived in a nice house. I also had three or four sets of new clothes. However, I no longer had my friends David and Peaches, and I was separated from Tina and my beloved Peggy. My separation anxiety was constant and overwhelming.

In one weekend, I had gone from a black elementary school with black nuns, living in an all-black neighborhood, to a white elementary school, with students and nuns who were white, and living in a racially mixed neighborhood. My psyche was crushed, I cursed God. I was living with people I do not know. That weekend probably cemented my belief that I simply could not trust anyone in life, including God.

After several weeks, I faced reality. I was still one of the smartest students in my class, and I competed against a female, who I had identified as an equal brainiac, Mareeka. She was always prepared, she was articulate, she was confident, and she was white.

I regret that I never got to know her. She would be surprised to know that she was my standard of academic excellence. On the boy's side, there was George who was head and shoulders above everyone. When the nun would ask a question that no one could answer, George could. At Nativity Elementary School, I met my first Asians, a Chinese brother and sister, Tommy and Corrine. Both were very nice, but a group of white boys consistently harassed them.

One day I had enough, and I said to these dudes, "Why don't you leave them alone?"

This group of four guys said, "Ni***r, we will kick your ass if you don't get out of here. Why are you protecting these slant-eyed yellow people?"

I was mad, but I was cool in my response, "My friends, you are white racist dogs and the reason you attack them as a group is because they are defenseless, and you are scared to do it as individuals. So, if you bother them again, I will look for you individually and we will have a serious discussion." Tommy and Corrine never had a problem after that.

I generally kept to myself at school, but I decided I would get involved in other things. At that time, I made the decision to become an altar boy, I guess because I was immersed in my Catholic school education and because one of the priests had asked me to. There were two priests who would play football with us and/or talk to the boys about school and about growing up. Another priest, who I will not name, made me and other altar boys uncomfortable. I had no problems with him until one day when he decided to test me. I watched him wrestle with some of the other altar boys as he tickled them, it appeared to me that he was fondling their genitals. I never would wrestle with him.

One Saturday afternoon, I was the lone altar boy, who was the server at afternoon mass and this particular priest was saying mass. After mass was over, I was putting things away in the sanctuary, when he spoke to me.

"Alan, you are one of the few altar boys who knows the entire mass in Latin. Most of the other altar boys do not, so I wanted to acknowledge that, but tell me, why is it that you do not interact with me like you do with the other priests?"

"Because I trust them and so do the other altar boys."

"You don't trust me?" he said incredulously. "What have I done to betray your trust?"

"Father I am going to be honest with you. I watch you wrestle with the other boys and then you start tickling them, tickling them in their crotch and feeling them up. These little white boys are too naïve to know what is really happening, but I am from the streets and I know what you are doing."

Slyly he responded, "Well, why don't we get to know each other now," as he reached for my shoulder. "You are not supposed to question your priest, are you?"

I slowly backed away from him and as he approached, I start throwing things at him. I threw the chalice that holds the wine, I threw the wafers that are used for communion, and I picked up a metal cross and threw it at him. At that point, I ran out the door exiting the church. I ran over to the convent to tell the nuns what Father had been doing because I knew they would believe me. I banged on the door and one of the older nuns answered. I proceeded to tell her that Father was a pervert, who fondled the altar boys and who had just tried to get next to me.

Her face flushed, she started screaming at me, "You are lying, you are a liar. Father would never do that."

I backed away from the door and looked at a few of the young nuns who had also come to the door. I could not believe that the nuns had betrayed me. That had never happened before. The black nuns at Saint Augustine's always had my back. I thought that these white nuns were protecting this white man.

The older nun continued, "I want you to go over there now and apologize to him."

I said, "No damn way will I apologize to that pervert."

I was now so hurt, that my eyes filled with tears. I turned away and started running down Georgia Avenue crying. I must have run twelve city blocks before I was exhausted. I did not go to school the following Monday or Tuesday. One of the younger nuns saw me on Wednesday and asked me to come to her classroom.

No one was there. She told me that her and some of the younger nuns believed me because a couple of altar boys, had told them how that priest made them uncomfortable.

I asked, "Why didn't you come to my defense? You just let that old nun beat me down."

She looked embarrassed as she told me that the older nuns would have been angry with her and any young nuns who supported my story. They feared retribution from her.

I looked at the nun and coldly said, "But it was alright for me to suffer and not you? What about the other altar boys who are being molested?"

She offered no answer or explanation. For the first time in my life, I doubted the integrity of the nuns.

CHAPTER 17
THE MIRACLE ON JEFFERSON STREET

After a period, the Anderson's trusted me enough that I was allowed to explore the neighborhood. My primary target was Rudolph Playground where some of the best young basketball players gathered. I knew that playing there would improve my skills quickly. The playground was literally one block from the Anderson's house, and as I walked towards it, I noticed something peculiar about midway down the block.

At one house an older white woman sat on her porch sofa, and she was talking to several young Black males situated on the sofa and the stairs. I was stunned at this picture, but I assumed there was logical explanation. I learned that this woman helped to feed some of these males when they were young kids and helped them with their homework. In return these kids cut her grass, went to the grocery store for her, and fixed things at her house. I learned that her kindness was rewarded by these young males as they became her protectors, and in a sense, her grandchildren.

Even though gentrification was gradually producing a predominantly Black neighborhood, she refused to be uprooted.

Some 50 years later, I became the Chancellor at Fayetteville State University (NC), and I met a White male who indicated that the older woman was his grandmother. He and other family members tried to get her to move from her residence in DC. He said her response was consistent, and it was that she did not want to abandon her grandchildren (the young Black males). She stayed in that house until she passed away.

Around this same time, I noticed that when I played sports, my muscles would ache afterwards for hours. This pain was over my entire body, not localized to any area. One night, I was laying on my adopted parent's bed, watching TV with them as I described this pain that I had been experiencing. They gave me a couple of aspirin and I went to bed.

The next morning, I heard the telephone ring in their bedroom. I pulled back the covers so that I could get up to answer the phone. Both of my adopted parents were at work, and I knew one of them was calling to wake me. As I stood, I took one step forward and fell uncontrollably, on my face. I tried to get up and could not. It felt as if my legs were paralyzed. I crawled on the floor to the phone and as I answered, I told my mother that I could not walk, and my muscles hurt all over my body. I just laid on the floor and waited until my father arrived; he rushed me to the hospital. I must have stayed in the hospital, about four days,–sleeping most of the time. Soon, I was allowed to return home and immediately became bedridden.

During the period when I first contracted rheumatic fever, I was introduced to a married couple who lived diagonally across the street from the Andersons. Dr. Cato (wife) and Dr. Strudwick (the husband) were movers and shakers in the Washington, DC medical community. Because of my young age, Dr. Cato became my pediatrician and was assisted by her husband. They both became very frustrated with my lack of progress as the rheumatic fever continued to accelerate.

Dr. Cato and I developed a close relationship (she is listed as one of my Surrogate Mothers at the end of the book).

Mr. and Mrs. Anderson were beside themselves and cried every day. Around my third day at home, they came into my room and told me that the doctors felt that there was nothing more they could do. In essence, it was their judgement that if the fever did not decrease, then I would surely die. They were so certain that this would happen that a catholic priest was called to come and give me the last rites, which he did. It seemed like an exorcism.

From my bed, I could stare out of the window, but the only thing that I saw was the top of trees. As time passed that evening, I could feel my life literally slipping away from me. It's such a strange feeling, that's difficult to put into words, but I sensed my body was ready to give up. I started doing what people often do when they are dying: I began to bargain with God. I uttered, "God, if you let me live, I will become a priest, or I will raise a lot of money for your Church. God, I promise I will stay celibate until I get married." I even chuckled to myself after I said this statement. My most sincere prayers were reserved for the Blessed Virgin Mary, who I had adopted years earlier, as the mother that I never had. There is a prayer to her that I have said since I was a child, and I now repeated it over and over:

MEMORARE

Remember,
O most gracious Virgin Mary,
that never was it known
that anyone who fled to thy protection,
implored thy help,
or sought thine intercession
was left unaided.
Inspired by this confidence, I fly unto thee,
O Virgin of virgins, my mother

to thee I do come,
before thee I stand, sinful and sorrowful.
O Mother of the Word incarnate, despise
not my petitions,
but in thy clemency
hear and answer me.
Amen

Since that time, whenever I have faced adversity in life, I would say this prayer. On this night, with life oozing away, I said this prayer over and over. I was afraid to fall asleep because I was afraid that I would not wake up, but I was so tired that I drifted into a semi-conscious state when suddenly, *THERE STOOD THE VIRGIN MARY.* Was I hallucinating? She smiled and reached over and touched my hand and said everything will be fine. In the morning my fever began to recede and in two days it had reverted to normal.

Everyone, especially the doctors, said this was simply a miracle. I have been haunted, in a good way, by the events of that night. Perhaps I am suffering from the curse of intellectuals, that is, we always try to identify rational explanations for events that we can't explain. Whatever the case, I survived and in my mind the Virgin Mary was the cause of my recovery. I almost died and then I was reborn. Mr. and Mrs. Anderson were so relieved, and I was happy for them.

Apparently, the virus that causes rheumatic fever can also instigate polio. Hence, just as I recovered fully from the fever, I contracted polio for a year and had to walk with those clunky braces. My life's tragedies seemed to never end, but there actually was a silver lining to these events.

The heart murmur associated with rheumatic fever prevented me from getting drafted into the military later during my college years, and I am forever grateful for that outcome. I did not get sent to Vietnam, unlike one of my best friends, Rick, who stepped on a land mine – they only found his hand. Apparently, no one told his mother about the nature of his death. The military authorities, only told her he had passed away, heroically, in the line of duty.

I was faced with the dilemma of telling her the truth or not. I went to visit her just to commiserate and I saw the suffering she was experiencing. If I told her about the "hand," it would only exacerbate her pain. So, I did not. Rick was one of my few close friends and when I learned about his manner of death, I cried for days. In my bewildered existence, I was once again, abandoned by someone I sincerely cared about.

CHAPTER 18
THE URBAN CLASSROOM

I had committed to becoming an awesome basketball player and excellent student. At Rudolph playground, some serious basketball was played, black kids and some older dudes hung out there.

It was there that I fell in love with basketball and I continued to hone my game years after that, such that I was awarded the status of an all-City player in Washington, DC. I was even given a B-ball nickname by other players. It was 'Ice Cream' because my game was cool and smooth like real ice cream. The playground was also a learning lab; that is, we were exposed to a range of activities – some innocuous, some questionable, some illegal, and many dangerous.

At the Rudolph playground, I was also introduced to a new gang that was feared, called the Decatur Street Boys. I made up my mind quickly that I wanted to roll with them. After all, one always needs protection.

The playground was only two blocks from my house thus, I had easy access to it. I also identified with a particular gang member, Michael, also known as "Punchy." It did not matter to me that he worked in construction and did not go to college because he was cool, handsome, respected by everyone, and he could fight. I witnessed three separate fights of his and in each case, the dude he fought was much bigger than him. I also got to know other members:

Superman, Calhoun, Pie, Derrick & Junior, Ham, Elwich and Bernard who tried to intimidate everybody. Bernard tried to intimidate the wrong person and ended up occupying a coffin. No one really cared, because he was disliked by most of us.

At each playground, there were unwritten rules or codes that had to be followed. For example, one day a group of us from Rudolph playground went to Raymond playground to play a touch football game.

We warmed up, and just as the game was to begin, one of the opposing players pointed to someone who was closing the gate to the only entrance or exit, and then he said bluntly, "If you win the game, then you don't leave."

Obviously, we played our worst game ever and we were all home in time for dinner.

A similar situation occurred at another playground. This time we went to play basketball against the Ridge Road Boys in Northeast DC. The rumor mill had portrayed them as intimidating thugs yet excellent ballers. As in the previous scenario, we were informed before the game, that we better not attempt to talk to any of the girls in attendance, and we didn't. After the game was over, we jumped into our two cars and sped off. I would like to say that we never did that to visitors at our home playground, Rudolph, but the reputation of the Decatur Street boys was well known throughout the city, so we didn't have to.

Two events occurred at Rudolph playground that would have a significant impact on my life. The first event involved a small group of black men, who would always be over at one end of the B-ball court gambling. Some were regular Rudolph guys, and some were often strangers who hunted out gambling scenarios whenever they could. Several of them were bona fide criminals.

One evening, while we were playing basketball, we could hear the gamblers talking smack. Suddenly one of them shouted to another gambler,

"Ni***r, you have been cheating, I been watching you."

He continued to rant, "You've been palming a pair of loaded dice and you exchange those for the regular dice."

In a swift move, the accuser brandished a straight razor and sliced the throat of the cheater. As the blood gushed out of his neck, the gamblers all started hauling ass in every direction.

Someone said, "He's dead, he's dead."

A couple of us ran over to see if we could help him. He was limp, laying in a pool of blood. As I stared at him, I told myself that this is what happens to those who live in the fast lane, gambling, pimping, gang banging and selling drugs. I realized that I wanted no part of that life, and no longer wanted to belong to the Decatur Street boys. Reputation and security be damned, fear had taken over. I would never hurt my adopted mother and father by getting into serious trouble.

The second event involved one of the ladies who periodically worked at the playground. When it was too hot to play B-ball or when it was raining, the recreation center would open, and we would play cards, ping pong, and board games like Scrabble or Jeopardy.

Over the months, I got to know the employees who were college students. The males I did not care for because they seemed elitist, and they looked down on us. My favorite female employee was the opposite. Her actions sought to encourage us to do positive things with our lives.

She especially showed me attention and tried to convince me that I had nothing in common with these gang members, and to use education as a platform for success in life. My boys used to tease me that she was sweet on me despite being six years older. One late afternoon, we were playing serious B-ball in a tournament that invited the best players from other playgrounds. In the middle of the game, she walked onto the court, and I immediately heard guys say,

"Get off the court B**ch, "B**ch, who do you think you are, somebody kick her ass off the court."

Ignoring them she walked over to me and took me by the hand and escorted me off the court.

She was looking very attractive that day and now comments were directed toward me, "Yo Alan, what you gonna do with that?" "She likes young boys, watch out man she will chain you in her basement."

As we exited the court, I asked her why she had embarrassed me in front all those brothers.

Sweetly, she said, "I just wanted you to walk me home." I responded, "I'm not your man or boyfriend, where is he?"

"I don't have a boyfriend and I chose you to walk with me. Is that alright?" Her sweet smile was so alluring.

Trying to sound like I was doing her a favor, I said "Ok, this one time, I will."

As we walked up North Capitol Street, she asked me a lot of questions and she was articulate just like you expect a college student to be.

"Do you have a girlfriend or special lady?" she asked.

I responded, "No, why are you asking?"

"Alan you are too young to see this now, but because you are smart, handsome, witty, and athletic, you will have a lot of women come on to you. How will you know who the right one is?" Have you had sex with a woman?"

"Yes" I responded. I knew I was lying but was embarrassed to admit I was a virgin.

"Was she someone you cared for?"

"I guess I must have liked her. I must have because I had sex with her."

"Alan, I can tell you are not being truthful, but don't be embarrassed. I just want you to really enjoy it your first time. I have grown to like you because you are such a sweet boy who sometimes tries to have a tough guy image. You have had a hard life."

I then said to her: "You are a woman, and I am just a teenager. Why me?" No response.

We arrived at her house, and she looked at me and asked, "Are you coming in?"

Though I was unsure, I gave in and walked inside. The rest is history. Sex, my first time, and it was all she said it would be. She was gentle and caring and guided me with no intimidation. At first, I was nervous touching a naked woman, but after a while it seemed like a natural part of everything else. She kissed me on my cheek and told me to remember this day. I left and as I walked down the street, I felt ten feet tall and felt a glow all around me. I hope every man gets a chance to be treated that way, if not the first time, at least at some point, I thought. For the first time in my life, I now felt like a man. From that point forward, she did not acknowledge that she had educated me in the bedroom.

She was still sweet and friendly, but every time I brought up what we did, she simply said, "It is not going to happen ever again. I just wanted it to be right for you the first time. Never settle for anything less."

Her rejection was difficult, but I understood her actions and over time, I accepted that we would only be friends.

The Decision

Over time, I learned that the Anderson's really were in the dark about Peggy. They were a very nice, caring couple from North Carolina. In an affectionate way, they both were very country, not sophisticated nor well educated, but they both were so happy that I had been delivered into their lives. They did not have much money, so I seldom asked for anything so they could pay their bills. I even found two little jobs: one at a bowling alley and one at a Chinese restaurant, and in both cases I would clean up after closing time.

I tried not to be too much trouble for my parents, but sometimes I stayed out all night without telling them. I was hanging out with my boys engaging in some mischief.

I developed a couple of friendships that brought me out of my shell. They were with playground friends: Mike, Chalmers, and Joe. As I grew older, I thought about what high school I wanted to attend. Two events on the same day pointed me in the direction of a particular high school. I was exiting the eighth grade, and one hot day, as I was walking home from school, I encountered several men with jackhammers digging up the street.

I stood and watched them for a minute, when an old black man who was sweating profusely turned to me and said, "Son, you don't want to spend your life doing what I am doing, working hard for little pay, so stay in school and work your ass off."

I have never forgotten that scene. I became even more inspired to succeed in school. The second event occurred when I had to change buses on my way home from school. As I was waiting to catch my second bus, I noticed three white males who were also waiting. They were students who wore uniforms like those worn by young men who attended West

Point. I went up to them and asked them if they were from the U.S. Military Academy at West Point, and if so, what were they doing at this bus stop.

They laughed and said, "No little man, we are students at St. John's high school up on Military Road."

From that moment on, I knew I would attend St. John's. The uniforms and the gleaming sword at their side had won me over. St. John's was a private Catholic college prep high school. My boys wanted me to go to the public high school, Roosevelt, with them. Most of the Decatur Street boys also attended that high school and I didn't want to get into any trouble hanging with them.

During the last week of school, I began to feel a little sad that I was leaving Nativity school, but I was so excited about attending St. John's. I walked down to Sister Euthalia's classroom to say goodbye. We laughed about our difficult encounter that first day when I was dropped off. Then she handed me a parting gift, a book. She said I had a difficult adjustment to Nativity school and a white environment, but I persisted and worked hard. In essence, I had recouped and become one of her prized students. The book was about the invasion of Europe by the African Moors and the cultural excellence that they had established there.

She said to me, "You are descended from African kings and scholars, and you need to learn about that. In the Catholic church we do not talk enough about the black Madonna, the child, and their presence in European churches. As you read, see yourself among the pages."

I thanked her, hugged her, and as I walked away, I realized how little I knew about Black/African history. This was a seminal moment for me, not only because of the contents of the book, but because I sensed that she saw something in me that I had not seen in myself. I read that book in two weeks and felt inspired and empowered. I was left with the question:

How did this white nun learn about the Moors and their impact on Europe? I wondered whether she shared this information with the white students. They probably would not even care. In retrospect, it was that gift from Sister Euthalia, that ignited my curiosity about the history of my race. This event influenced my later involvement in the Civil Rights movement, the Black Power movement, The Women's Liberation Movement, and the Global Liberation movement.

I read everything I could after that into young adulthood. I developed a personal library and continued to read about black history to strengthen my identity. That same identity was amorphous before I began devouring books. When I was in college, I was introduced to another book that I identified with. It was titled *Manchild in the Promised Land* by the author, Claude Brown. It was a searing expose on the difficult upbringing of a Black male who lived in a treacherous urban environment.

When I finished the book, I read it again, and I realized that I had been the "man-child" of Corcoran Street. I did recognize that the outcomes in life for young black males who face adversity are vastly different. Fortunately, I had been delivered from a perilous outcome, primarily by the women, who had touched my life. I easily could have fallen into the pit of infamy and ended up dead, in prison, or became a con man or a professional criminal.

As I got older, I realized that my escape and deliverance over time was due to a higher power who surrounded me with angels.

CHAPTER 19
THE FEMALE PILLARS OF MY SURVIVAL IN THIS NEW REALITY

I have previously described the pain and fear that I experienced because of the infamous "Snatch in the Night." The strong, debilitating emotions that could have lingered for months and years were mollified by the presence of three individuals who, from the time of our initial interactions, sought only to care for and about me.

I was too young to understand that they provided me with a life-saving elixir, that prevented me from descending into a debilitating depression. They were in my life from the time I arrived at the Anderson's home, all through high school, and saw me off to college. They became my emotional anchors. A very nice, older couple, lived next door to the Anderson's and their houses were attached.

The wife, Mrs. Toney, was very supportive of me and took an interest in my well-being for years. I created the image of her as the grandmother that I never had. I never established a close relationship with her husband, Mr. Toney, although we were always cordial to one another. The incredible blessing of my relationship with Mr. and Mrs. Toney, was accentuated by my relationship with their three granddaughters.

After I first arrived at the Anderson's home, I would sit on the front porch for long stretches at a time, still stunned by the events that brought me there.

One day, a female about my age emerged from the Toney's house, stood on her porch, and greeted me. She invited me to come over to have lunch with her and her two sisters. She told me her name, and she seemed to be so sweet. The lunch was scheduled for the next day and I was nervous about attending. Was this another surprise? Was this part of the whole scheme of kidnapping that brought me there? Were Mr. and Mrs. Toney and the granddaughters going to keep tabs on me, and report back to Mr. and Mrs. Anderson? My mind was primed to be skeptical of everyone and everything, because just weeks before, I had been kidnapped. I had no idea what I was going to talk to them about, during lunch.

After agreeing to the invitation, I went inside to tell Mr. and Mrs. Anderson to alert them that I had no clothes to wear, other than what I had arrived with. We went shopping shortly after that, but we had a disagreement about the clothes I should buy. They had a prep-like perspective on how I should dress, and I still had the "street boy" perspective, so we sort of met half-way.

The next day, I was greeted by Mrs. Toney with her effervescent smile at the door and went to lunch. She told me to go downstairs and meet her granddaughters. In retrospect, I was very nervous, and my heart was pounding. In addition to Peggy, the prostitutes were the only other women that I learned to care about. As I reached the bottom of the stairs, the three of them greeted me enthusiastically, indicating that they were happy that I now lived next door.

It was so interesting to watch. The three of them sought to make me feel comfortable, and despite how hesitant I was to accept their efforts, I was still appreciative of their attempt. I can't remember what we talked about, but I was glad that they did not try to pry into my life. I could tell from their questions that they really did not know much about how I arrived at 201 Jefferson Street, N.W. In fact, they thought that I chose to leave my previous life to come live with the Anderson's.

We had sandwiches, chips, and iced tea. They waited on me and made me feel special, which was so important because my self-worth was at rock bottom. They asked me why I chose to live with Mr. and Mrs. Anderson, and I simply responded that it was not my choice. They asked how it felt to be adopted, and I could not answer. I was not aware of that possibility, nor had I heard it mentioned. I realized that I needed to ask the Andersons about that. If I were legally adopted, then why did I have to be kidnapped?

Over time, I began to warm up to the three granddaughters, as we had many more lunches, and we even began to play softball in the alley behind our houses. One granddaughter and I had a close relationship, but I was not used to having feelings for a young woman other than Peggy. I recognized that I had strong feelings for this granddaughter but did not know how to express them. Moreover, my plan at that time, was to run away and find my way back to Corcoran Street.

One Saturday, the four of us were playing hide and seek at their house. The daughter who I was close to was the seeker, trying to locate the three of us, which in a house with three floors was a challenge. She found me hiding in the basement and as I stood, I was disappointed that I was identified so quickly.

After that, I grew closer to all three sisters, and we started spending more time together. We went to the movies at the neighborhood Kennedy Theater and just hung out. Once the lure of the playground and the streets captured my time and attention, I spent less time with the three angels. As I became more proficient at basketball, I realized that to become a star, I had to give more time to that. I played twice a day every day, and only took a break to go home and eat.

Then that fateful day arrived, when that particular female walked onto the B-ball court, and took me by the hand, so I could walk her home. Once I started attending St. John's High School, I was drawn into a new reality that now included challenging academic courses and increased time studying. I also played basketball and football and attended practices for both.

I began attending house parties and meeting new people, especially young ladies. I ceased thinking about running away as I got older, but I never stopped thinking about Peggy. That fall, I met a female named Narine. She approached me in my sophomore year of high school, after I had played very well in a basketball game against our hated rival, DeMatha High School. Narine talked to me in a very mature manner and asked if we could go out. She suggested that she could pick me up from St. John's after school on Monday around 3:30 p.m. I had never been approached by a female who talked to me in such an assertive manner. She was on time and as we drove away from school, I noticed that she had a few French language magazines in the back seat. I picked one up and saw that it was really written in French.

I asked her why she was reading those. She said she had a desire visit Paris one day and wanted to learn the language. We had a pleasant rest of the day and she drove me home. I sat in my room that night and understood that Narine was a mature woman. I had to step my game up so I would not bore her. It was an awakening that I needed to experience and value. Now, I had to face the next level up in my manhood status. We dated for a few years and established an unbreakable, loving friendship based on trust, that sustained us long after we ended the romance.

In retrospect, I am thankful that another woman had loved, cared for me, and contributed to my growth as a man. I was always fascinated that she could tell me things that I didn't know. Three decades after we first met, Narine told me that I was depressed when she met me in high school and that it continued into manhood. She also said that I was afraid to really love her or any woman for that matter.

She then said something stunning – that I lived my love life through romantic love songs because it was safer than to trust a woman with my heart. She understood that the issue was not my fear of women, rather it was the sum of all fears that had punctuated my existence since birth. I thought about her revelation for many years, until I realized, with great uneasiness, that it was true.

I never shared completely with Narine, during those intervening years, the episodes of emotional hurt and pain that I had experienced; that all had an additive effect. We both were attached to similar love songs: The first one, was my self-proclaimed theme song concerning the absence of love in my life, and the other two, spoke to her exhaustive attempts to gain my trust and open my heart to her.

Narine was right about one thing; I lived my romantic life through romantic love songs. Unbeknownst to them, I often attached songs to females in a way that defined the nature of my relationship with them. Once when I was sixteen years old, I was riding my bicycle in Rock Creek Park with a friend, as we passed an area known as the Carter Baron Amphitheater, where outdoor concerts were held, I could hear someone singing, and the voice was pure and heavenly. I did not know the lyrics to many of the songs, but I was entranced by the romanticism that they projected.

Bobo and I rode our bikes over to the entrance of the amphitheater and asked the ticket taker who was singing.

He said, "Johnny Mathis."

I stayed longer to listen, but Bobo left to head home. We were both deep into Motown music and sang with different local bands, usually at high school dances. I was so enthralled with the voice and music of Johnny Mathis, that I immediately rode my bike to the record store and bought my first album, *Johnny Mathis Greatest Hits*. Five decades later, I have fifty-eight of his albums and have seen him perform eight times.

My second high school romance, during my senior year was brief, but exceedingly intense. I met her at a house party, and it was the classic love at first sight. I called her and thought about her every day. Although she cared for me, I could tell that she wanted and needed some distance periodically. Of course, I could not see then, that the intensity of my feelings for her, were rooted in my need to be loved by a mother. I also could not see that I was smothering her.

There also was another issue that I blew out of proportion. She lived in a section of Washington, D.C., known as the Gold Coast. It was a wealthy section of upper Northwest 16th street. We teens who did not live amid such wealth, always felt we were looked down on by the Black Bourgeoisie from the Gold Coast. They went to the best schools, and most had their own cars to drive. When I first went to visit her to meet her parents, I was questioned by her father-in-law, who did not want his daughter to date a commoner, especially one who had been abandoned by his real parents.

To please him, she began to withdraw from me gradually. I was caught in the rush of passion and the teenage daily pining for that unreachable love. Within six months, I had descended into a brutal pit of disillusionment and despair. She tried to warn and tell me that her reality was taking her in a different direction in life.

At the end of our senior year, we attended different universities, but I continued to pursue her. Because her real father lived in Columbus, Ohio, she attended Ohio State University, and I attended Villanova University near Philadelphia. I persisted in asking her if I could visit her, and in a calm, reasonable way, she asked me not to come. I should have listened. Her love for me did not fade; rather, she never really loved me the way I longed for. She cared for me all the while managing my desperate obsession. She gave in and allowed me to visit her, and it was clear that she had a new group of friends, and even a boyfriend. Her real father, who was suave and cool, tried to reassure me that my life would go on successfully without his daughter, and I needed to let her go.

When it was time to leave Ohio, I told her that I knew it was over, and I would not return. I can't forget that dark, lonely train ride from Columbus to Philadelphia. I cried depressing tears the entire way back to campus and my dorm room. I slept eleven hours. When I awoke, I looked in the bathroom mirror and almost screamed. My perfectly smooth facial skin was now covered with ugly acne. What had begun to me as hope, had now descended into pathos.

I did not call Rene to tell her about my physical reaction to the end of the relationship. I recognized that this outcome was not her fault. I completely accepted responsibility for my desperate, immature, and naïve infatuation with a beautiful angel. I remember that I once asked she why she liked me and why she spent time with me. Her answer was that I was a cute rogue – I guess she was infatuated with a handsome 'bad boy.' This 'trail of tears' would haunt me for decades as any romance became my emotional straight jacket. My main man, Chuck, tried to counsel me through my obsession with her, but I would not listen. As was the case with previous girlfriends, I was betrayed by my obsessive need, to be loved by a mother, and my failed attempts to find that with girlfriends was always doomed to fail. I also thought about a relationship with a young woman who I met at an amusement park in Hersey Park, PA. Fortunately, she only lived five city blocks from me, thus it was easy to visit her.

We truly liked each other, but two issues prevented us from growing closer. One issue was that she was the daughter of a prominent pastor who was known for his emotional preaching style but always seemed suspect of my motives. I guess he perceived me as another young black man trying to hit on the daughter he was trying to protect. The other issue was that she had a baby girl, and she was skeptical of men and relationships.

I tried to convince her that I would care for her and her daughter, but she felt I would forget about her when I went to college. For these and other reasons, we drifted apart, and it might have been better for her that we did since I was confronting my own demons. I simply wish I was able to see her again to let her know how much I cared for her during my troubled times.

CHAPTER 20
MY EXPANDING FAMILY

Mrs. Anderson had a sister, Aunt Mattie, and she lived not too far away on 822 Decatur Street, NW. I spent a lot of time there in the summers because the Anderson's did not trust me to be at home alone. I forfeited that right a few weeks earlier, I threw a day party where about forty adolescents attended. It was a great party in the basement, but I had to keep my eye on some of the dudes that I did not know. They kept trying to sneak upstairs probably to see what they could steal.

After everyone left, I was joined by Mike and Chalmers who helped me to clean up. My parents never suspected a thing until a neighbor across the street gave me up. I was on punishment for two weeks, which amounted to being at home when I was not in school and no phone calls. The latter bothered me, because I had recently met a female named Thomasina, and I could not even call her on the phone.

She and I never really got to know each other, but she is memorable for another reason, and I even created an identification moniker for her. I used to tell her that she wore 'Killer' jeans because she was blessed with 'Killer' genes. Her body and every curve associated with it were perfectly poured into those jeans. Upon seeing her in those jeans, most men would first gasp and then keep on staring. The best pair of fitted jeans that I have ever been blessed to observe on a woman.

Sometimes, you simply must appreciate God's aesthetic creations.

Aunt Mattie had a son who was a big-time ladies' man. His name was Kirk and he seemed obsessed with women. He was dating a friend of mine for a few years after she graduated from high school. He was in his forties, and she was in her early twenties. Kirk married a woman named Fannie and they had two daughters. They were present when I came to live with the Anderson's. Over time, I grew to love Fannie, and I saw her as the mother I always wanted. Her daughters became the sisters that would replace Peggy in my life. Kirk was evil, selfish, and egocentric, and while married to Fannie, he cheated on her multiple times. In fact, he often used me as an excuse to engage in his affairs. He would tell his wife and mother that he was going to take me for a ride somewhere. We would end up at some woman's house, and I was told to watch TV while they slithered into the bedroom.

One day, I came over to Aunt Mattie's house and witnessed an ugly argument between Kirk and Fannie. He began to physically assault her and without thinking, I jumped on his back, and told him to leave her alone. I was about 15 years old. Kirk threw me to the floor, jumped on top of me, and began to punch me in the face like he would a grown man. He cursed me and told me to never interfere with him again. From that moment on, I convinced myself that I would never let someone assault me like that again.

Moreover, I told him that when I was older, I would get my revenge against him, and I did. It was that incident involving Fannie and Kirk that caused me to lose respect for my adopted mother and her sister, Aunt Mattie. After Kirk physically assaulted me, I lay on the floor, bloody and badly beaten. Aunt Fannie attempted to console me and proceeded to wipe the blood from my face.

As I stood, I asked Aunt Mattie why she did not tell her son to stop assaulting Fannie, and then me. She came up with some lame ass excuse about Kirk being upset, and that's when I realized she was justifying his actions.

I rode my bicycle home, and as I walked in, my mother said, "I just talked to Mattie, and she told me how you and Fannie had upset Kirk and caused him to lose his temper."

I went to my room and locked the door behind me. I realized that I had been betrayed by two women who I thought loved me, and it was because Kirk was the "golden child" who could do no wrong. I refused to interact with him after that, and my hatred for him continued to grow.

His daughters became my little sisters and served as emotional anchors for me, in the same way that the Toney sisters did. One sister and I have remained very close, and I love her to death. Later in life, the other sister tried to steal money from me, and we have not spoken since.

She forged a credit card in my name, and I am still in disbelief that she did that - hurt and betrayed again by someone I loved. It took a while for me to understand that this daughter had serious emotional problems. I had hoped that one or both daughters would replace my relationship with Peggy, but no one could do that.

CHAPTER 21
THE POLITICS OF MY BLACK IDENTITY

St. John's College High School (1962-1966) was a private, all-male college prep institution. It is Catholic and run by the Christian Brothers. When I attended, the enrollment was largely white and only about 10 % were black. We were spread across four grade levels (9-12); thus, at St. John's, we were seldom seen as a cluster.

Even the two dominant sports teams, football, and basketball, only had three or four blacks on each team. There

was a military emphasis at the institution. We had to wear a military uniform (that I loved), we had to compete for military rank (I was a Lieutenant), and we marched and drilled in formation early in the morning instead of the more traditional exercise periods. I guess that is how our school nickname emerged. We were known as the "CADETS.

Once again, I was attending a predominantly white school, with all white instructors, in a predominantly white neighborhood, but I lived in a predominantly black neighborhood. I will, however, be the first to testify, that the education that I received at St. John's was outstanding. I was very, well prepared, to attend Villanova University or any university. My drive to compete with the white students led to a healthy motivation. I had no feelings of inferiority, relative to those I competed against, rather it was a continuation of my drive toward excellence, that had been instilled by the Catholic nuns at St. Augustine's and Nativity schools.

I could confide in Brother Timothy and the R.O.T.C. leader, MSG Mike. There were 231 seniors in my graduating class, and only 12 were African Americans: James Anderson, David Booker, Joe Brighthaupt, Gary Cooper, Lorne Hill, Noble Jones, Gregory Lawson, Erskin Mackall, Michael Mebane, Melvin Parker, John Roxborough, and Charles Stewart. The year before, that number was cut in half. Despite our low numbers, the black students were treated with respect, and we easily assimilated in the culture of St. John's.

At St. John's H.S., I developed my first close friendship with a white student. He sat next to me in my homeroom class, and we talked about everything. He was the nicest person, and the friendship just clicked. His name was Stephen, and he was supportive of me academically and athletically. Unbeknownst to me, he attended different football and basketball games that I played in, and the next school day, we would discuss my performance. I didn't even know he had attended those events. In terms of academics, we would compare test results without any judgment whatsoever. We would discuss questions that we each got wrong, and then we would try to figure out the errors we made. I was very comfortable around Stevie and I felt I could trust him.

After graduation from high school, we lost contact, but his friendship was important for another reason. It counterbalanced my introduction to the Civil Rights movement and the Black Power movement. Many leaders in both movements often vocalized anti-white, anti-establishment sentiments and, in doing so, converted many young black men toward that line of thinking. I could have easily been lured into the anti-white politics of black nationalism, but my relationship with Stevie prevented that from happening. My real awakening occurred when I attended the historic March on Washington in August 1963.

The powerful words of Martin Luther King, Julian Bond, A. Phillip Randolph, and others led to my conversion to become a warrior in the army of Civil Rights and black Nationalism – FOREVER. However, I would not make public or private statements against white folk. I berated the systemic and structural racism that was at the root of racial and economic inequities between rich and poor of any race. I even berated many white and black leaders for their hypocrisy and failure to confront white America.

I wish I could tell Stevie about his impact on me. Maybe one day I will be able to, or maybe, he will have the opportunity to read this book. I have always been loyal to and supportive of St. John's high school. When I was asked to participate on the Board of Trustees, without hesitation, I accepted the invitation. As my comfort zone expanded, I began to see St. Johns as my first real family. A few years ago,

I received a call from the president of St. John's and was asked to pay half of the tuition for a star female basketball player, who existed in difficult family circumstances, as I did years before. Again, without hesitation, I agreed to assume that financial responsibility. Today, over half of the students are racial minorities, and there are several of us on the Board of Trustees.

During high school, I developed close friendships with two young African American men who attended St. John's. My relationships with Erskine "Tony" and Chuck "Clancy" have endured for about 50 years, because of our mutual respect and love, because we had the same sense of humor, because we were high school athletes, cared about one another and each other's families, we were academically sound, attended parties together, and because we were students with good values who lived in stable homes. What was most important, was that we were emerging from adolescence into young manhood. We were being exposed to the same external messages and cues about the politics of black identity. While we did discuss extreme incidents in the public domain, it was not until we began to attend college, that our understanding of complicated political issues began to mature.

I became very close emotionally to the families of Tony and Chuck. They were the siblings that I never had, and I trusted both. I was very sad when their mothers died because they treated me like their son.

Two other important African American males in my life attended other high schools. One is named Cyril and we have been life-long friends. We met in high school through a mutual female friend and went on to be roommates at Villanova University. Over time, we became trusted confidants. Cyril knows the emotional me more than anyone. His family accepted me as one of their own, and his younger sister, Tricia, has become my little sister. He has been the only person in my life who I have allowed to express any emotion to me, to ask any question, or to confront me when necessary, and I have taken his words to heart. He is also one of the nicest, most caring individuals that I have ever met.

Throughout my life, he has been the one I approached when I needed encouragement and guidance. He has been a male angel sent to look after me. Only once have I been angry with him when I felt he hurt or betrayed me by not revealing a secret. We have shared some incredible episodes in our lives, enough for another book. I am not too proud to say that I truly love that man and always will.

My fourth high school friend was Chalmers "the philosopher." He earned that nickname because he majored in philosophy in college. He dressed and acted differently from the rest of the guys who played basketball at the local playground. He would not curse and 'talk trash' like the rest of us, rather his comments were intellectual, observational, and philosophical. I admired that about him, but other young brothers found him odd. I often had to step in to defend him at the playground, when he argued with young males who possessed a street mentality, and who wanted to intimidate him. He often seemed oblivious to the potential danger that was about to consume him. I guess ignorance is really bliss.

My public support for more vocal Black leaders produced a serious clash of beliefs with Mrs. Anderson. My father was apolitical, and he was happy just smoking a cigar and watching Lawrence Welk or a baseball game on television. On the other hand, my mother criticized my support of black nationalists like Malcolm X, Roy Innis, Stokely Carmichael, and Angela Davis. She loved to point out that Malcolm X was a 'member of the Black Muslims.' She called them a racist, fanatical organization and said that I should subscribe to the nonviolent message of Roy Wilkins, the national leader of the NAACP.

I tried to show her historical information about the history of murder, lynching, and rape that was perpetrated against black people and the planned genocide of Native Americans, and that this could not be successfully addressed by non-violent protests. At some point in the argument, I would just walk out of the room. In retrospect, I sometimes wonder how I could have acted differently.

Walking out during a conversation with one's mother was so disrespectful, and I deeply regret those actions. She was rooted in her beliefs and those same beliefs matched those of her work environment and value system at the C.I.A.

When I began high school, I learned about this organization in D.C. known as PRIDE, INC., It provided young black males with their first job. It was created by former mayor Marion Berry, who was a legend in the black community, and who charged the PRIDE participants with a sense of accountability and ownership in terms of the city but especially for their own communities. The original PRIDE Inc. headquarters was located at 1536 U Street, N.W. Mr. Berry spent a good deal of time talking to us about black identity and black empowerment. The jobs were menial and often involved cleaning up the neighborhood or painting a building that needed refurbishing.

I was so proud when I wore my PRIDE INC. t-shirt, but it led to another argument with my mother when I returned home. She was not a supporter of Marion Berry, who she often referred to as, a thug. It is unfortunate that in his role as Mayor, Mr. Berry later succumbed to an addiction to crack cocaine, which became a public outrage, when his actions were taped and photographed in a downtown hotel.

The nightly news captured this moment of infamy in print and video. Marion Barry was portrayed as another man who had sold out his community, and he was exposed as weak, because he put his personal inclinations ahead of his responsibility to the city, especially the minority community. Compounding this indignity, was that he was set up and turned in by the woman he loved. Despite this moment of public infamy and humiliation, many members of the Black community continued to be vocal in their support of the mayor.

CHAPTER 22
MY EMBARRASSING MISPERCEPTION OF MY ADOPTED PARENTS

As I indicated earlier, my adopted parents were very simple people who had not gone beyond a high school education, and I related to them as such. I now recognize that I was remiss in terms of a deeper exploration of their respective personas. My father was born in 1901, during the transition period between post-slavery reconstruction and the embedding of Jim Crow laws in America. He possessed a historical memory of the life that Negro Americans labored under.

He was not the type of person to question any mistreatment or unfairness, and instead he just worked harder. If you did not know him, he could appear to be a jovial introvert, but I remember the times he returned home from work visibly angry with the way "Mister Charlie" had treated minority employees. I later learned that many old black men referred to white men as "Mister Charlie." I don't know the slave origins of the term, but it clearly had a negative connotation when applied to white men. His early life was as a sharecropper in Pitt County, North Carolina, and he was a god-fearing man loyal to his church and wife. They were married for 65 years, and they loved and respected one another every day of that marriage.

My mother was born Avor Catherine Anderson in LaGrange, North Carolina. In her career, she held two positions that elevated her to a special status among her peers. First, when the Central Intelligence Agency opened in 1947 in Langley, Virginia, they hired approximately 1800 new or reassigned employees. As one might expect, only a small percentage of them were African American. My mother was lucky to be one of those hired as an administrative secretary and her tenure was 1947 – 1971. As a testament to her value as a member of the intelligence community, when she retired, the Director of the CIA attended her going-away event, which he seldom did for other secretaries. He also presented her with the following letter:

Central Intelligence Agency
Office of the Director
12 April 1971

Mrs. Avor C. Anderson
201 Jefferson Street, N. W.
Washington, D.C. 20011

Dear Mrs. Anderson:

As you bring to a close more than twenty-seven years of service to your country (Navy Dept. and CIA), I want to join your friends and co-workers in wishing you well and hoping that you find the years ahead filled with enjoyment and satisfaction.
It takes the conscientious efforts of many people to do the important work of this Agency.
You leave with the knowledge that you have personally contributed to our success in carrying out our mission. Your faithful and loyal support has measured up to the high ideals and traditions of the Federal service.
May I express to you my appreciation and extend my best wishes for the years ahead.

Sincerely,

Richard Helms
Director

I regret that I did not express to my mother, my admiration and pride in her success. Moreover, in retrospect, I now better understand her loyalty to the Agency and the country, and why she expressed problems with the radical leaders of the Black Power Movement. At the time that I came to live with the Andersons, my mother was working at the Navy Department before she moved to the C.I.A.

Because of her level of security clearance, I was fortunate to have summer jobs for four consecutive years that included my last two years of high school and my first two years of college. To be eligible for summer employment, all the prospective students had to one, write a brief bio about oneself and then two, at a selected location take an in-person exam. Like other applicants, I was a junior in high school, and this is the exact letter that I submitted as an application:

James A. Anderson
201 Jefferson Street, N.W.
Washington, DC 20011

T-100 Headquarters Room 5E56

Attention: Kathy

I never realized how difficult it was for an author to write his or her biography until I was instructed to write merely three hundred words about myself and my future. My problem lies in retaining a reasonable degree of objectivity and accuracy. I guess when people write about themselves, they have a tendency, consciously or subconsciously, to present a most favorable, one-sided picture (of themselves). This tendency toward egocentrism is human nature, and I will try to sustain as objective an attitude as possible.

A physical description of myself is unimportant and just a few words will suffice. I am five feet and ten inches tall and weigh one hundred and sixty pounds. I am a very good athlete and prefer basketball over all other sports. The most important aspect of my physical being is the color of my skin; I am a Negro, and it is also one of the main sources of my motivations now and in the future. Emotionally, I am a very introspective person and I consider myself an individualist and often a semi-nonconformist. I am critical, yet happy-go-lucky. I worry too much about things, especially the racial situation at home and the Vietnam crisis abroad. Finally, I have been an honor student during my entire tenure at St. John's College High School in Washington, D.C.

As I mentioned before, because I am a Negro, I feel I have an obligation to myself, my race, and my country. I intend to major in psychology at Villanova University and hope to attend graduate school at either Princeton or Stanford University. One of the obstacles blocking my path to success may be the military draft. Assuming I don't get drafted, I hope to become a social psychologist or a child psychologist and work in one of the areas hospitals. I also plan to get married when I am about twenty-six years old. One of my other aspirations is to visit other countries and study their cultures. Also, I would like to try my hand at writing a book and becoming a public speaker."

In retrospect, I am amazed at how many of my predictions have been realized. Concerning the exam, I clearly remember that there were about fifty high school students taking the exam, and all were white except me. The test was not that difficult but it was a timed exam and that was the most taxing aspect of it. The students were told that we would be contacted in about a week with the results. When I was contacted, I was told that I was the first student called because I had scored the highest on the test, and could I come for a visit to discuss my summer options. I agreed and appeared on the required day.

When I arrived at my destination, I noted that there were about ten other students sitting in the waiting room, I presume, for the same reason that I was there. The government representative would come out and call a name and that student went into her office for a conversation. The other white students were called before I was, which upset me because I was told that I had scored the highest on the exam. When I finally sat down with the representative, I was asked how I thought I did on the exam. I responded that I felt that I did well, but she said not to get my hopes up.

She then looked at her list and fell silent and looked very puzzled and turned to me and said, "According to this list, you scored the highest on the exam, but that can't be correct."

I responded, "Why, can't that be correct, after all another person had called me and affirmed my first-place status and she did not know what I looked like."

She then said, "I assumed that it would be one of the other students that I interviewed before you."

I asked her why, since she had a verified list. Was she going to adhere to it? She finally gave me an honest response.

"I never thought a colored boy would outperform all the white students, especially on an exam that had a lot of math," she said nervously.

Confidently, I informed her that was a racist belief, and she should be ashamed to state that publicly. I informed her that Africans, Chinese and Indians (from India) invented mathematics.

And then, she said something that was unbelievable, "Would you mind taking the test again, to verify your score?"

My response was terse but strong and confident, "I will only do that if the other 49 white students also retake the test, and I want them to be told why this repeat of exam-taking was necessary."

I went home and told my mother, who suggested that I should do what these white people wanted, because I might not get the job and she might get some grief from the agency. It was clear that my mother cared more about the perceptions of white folks than my racist treatment by the representative. I learned a cruel reality that day, and it just affirmed that I had to stand strong in the face of challenges to my integrity, and intellect from a parent or a stranger.

The summer jobs were not that challenging, but this was the first time that I was exposed to a predominantly white working environment, especially one as prestigious as the CIA. I did learn about the 'Need to Know' principle of the C.I.A. because it was drilled into us regularly. Hence, I never sought out any information that I did not need to know

I had no plans to develop a career at a federal agency, hence I was quite surprised when I received a call from them as I neared completion of my Ph.D. at Cornell University. This was about 10 years since I first worked there. I was informed that there were few minority agents at the CIA, and since I previously had worked there, had a Ph.D., and had security clearance, then I was a most desired candidate.

I asked if they had been tracking me since I last worked there, because how would they know that I was finishing my Ph.D.? They indicated that they did check on me periodically. I asked about the expectations for me if I were to work there. For example, would I be expected to infiltrate or spy on black political/community organizations? I was told that might be one of my responsibilities.

My response was immediate: I would never do that to a black organization, and I was not interested in working there. In retrospect, this was my first political decision and response that suggested that my black identity was maturing.

As fate would have it, later in life, I worked as Vice President at Texas A&M university for three years (2006-2008) and I reported to then President, Robert Gates, the former head of the CIA and the National Security Agency. He was a mentor and friend, and he was very proud of my mother's service and mine at the CIA. When he was asked to return to Washington, D.C. to serve as the Secretary of Defense, by then President George Bush, he became very emotional, as he explained that he knew that some of us had only come to Texas A&M to work with him. I was in that category, and I quickly decided that I would leave Aggieland without President Gates there as our leader and my personal protector.

Dr. James A. Anderson

CHAPTER 23
MY ADOPTED MOTHER: A COMMUNITY ACTIVIST?

Mrs. Anderson belonged to a community women's organization, 'The Friendly Matrons Club.' In fact, she was a charter member who served as second Vice President. The club was formed on February 8, 1948, in Washington, DC, by ten community-minded women, who were primarily government workers.

Over the years, the organization's projects included donations, furnishings, gifts and services, entertainments, scholarships, and contributions. Among the recipients were The Children's Hospital, the Blue Plains Hospital for Senior Citizens, D.C. Village, Stoddard Baptist Home, St. Ann's Home, Cedar Knolls Training School, Northwest Settlement Home, Southwest Settlement Home, St. Elizabeth's Mental Health Hospital, Spingarn High School students, and the Frederick Douglass Home Restoration Fund.

The group met regularly and alternated the location of their gatherings at the homes of different members. A few weeks after the 'Snatch in the Night,' it was Mrs. Anderson's turn to host the meeting. Besides attending to their normal club business, this was also to be a showcase of Mrs. Anderson's new purported adopted son. I was not aware of this until I was called to interrupt my studying and come down to the living room to meet the members.

The first thing I remember is that they dressed up for the meeting as if they were going to church. After each club member introduced herself, they reminded me over and over how lucky I was to be "resurrected" from that tragic life that preceded my coming to live with Anderson. They asked me questions, but they were not ready for some of the answers.

For example, I was asked, "What do you want to be when you grow up?"

My response was quick and to the point, "I used to think I knew until I was kidnapped, now I'm not sure, what's going to happen next in my future."

Dead silence followed! Many of the members assumed that I had experienced a normal adoption process.

After my adopted parents passed away in 1994 (6 months apart, I learned more about my mother's involvement with the Friendly Matron's Club. I was stunned to learn that the club worked with a local black church, and the goal was to unionize housekeepers in D.C. They would meet the housekeepers at bus stops and distribute literature to them. My perceptions of them as a group of concerned but bourgeois old ladies began to change, and I felt guilty about the limited picture I had created. I wish I had known this then, as I do now, because I would have approached my interactions with them differently. Unfortunately, I am still having difficulty with something else I discovered, as I reviewed my parent's papers after their death. I started to read a legal document which certified my formal adoption by Mr. and Mrs. Anderson.

I had falsely assumed that my legal adoption occurred shortly after I came to live with them, but I was a sophomore in college when my adoption was consummated nine years later (1967). I was even more confused because someone had fabricated, and given to my adopted parents, a birth certificate that listed them as my original parents.

HOW COULD I HAVE BOTH DOCUMENTS? How can a young person be identified as being with parents since birth, and yet be adopted by them some 17 years later? What I have discovered since then, is that a lawyer who was a family friend, handled both actions. He passed away and his law firm (Malley & Newton) has dissolved, hence, I am not able to investigate this contradictory situation. Somehow, he knew about me in my prior life and made the arrangements for me to live with the Andersons. Apparently, my adopted mother, Mrs. Anderson, had three miscarriages and she and her husband were desperate to have a child. Enter, the Newton law firm.

My name on the birth certificate was James Allen Anderson. I had never heard that name until I came to live with these people. Somehow, I retained both documents as evidence of the circuitous route of my life.

The Final Decree of Adoption lists that it (# 683-66) was filed on October 21, 1966, and was granted on March 17, 1967. It was signed by Judge Joseph M. F. Ryan, Jr. The document states: 'It is further ORDERED that JAMES ALLEN ANDERSON shall henceforth be the official name of the said Adoptee.'

This document certifies that I had no legal standing with the Andersons for my first nine years with them. I asked an older lawyer about this, and he said that back then, families just passed around Black children without any legal concerns. I guess the schools that I attended didn't care about completely certifying my legal existence, rather they allowed the fake birth certificate to be the primary source of evidence.

Why do I want to know more about this situation? Because somewhere in this discovery process, I was/am hoping to learn the identities of my birth parents. Shortly after the discovery of the adoption paper (which was devoid of any signatures of my birth parents), I visited what was then called the Bureau of Vital Statistics in DC (formerly on 6th street NW) where original copies of certificates were housed. I assumed that on that document, would be the identities of at least one of my birth parents. I walked into the appropriate office and filled out the request form and, as others were doing, I submitted it to the clerk.

As time passed other names were called to pick up their official birth certificate, and I began to wonder what had caused the delay with my materials. A woman emerged from another office and called my name, and I went in to meet with her. I had taken copies of the funeral programs for each of my adopted parents, who passed 6 months apart, to support my request for my original birth certificate. I will never forget her comments to me:

"Sir, I always feel so bad when individuals like you are trying to identify something about their past, especially who are their parents. In your case, as in many others, unfortunately when you were adopted, the courts had your papers sealed for 50 years, hence you cannot obtain your original birth certificate until then."

I asked if that was 50 years from my birth or from my official adoption, and I was told it was the latter.

I then asked how I might be able to get my papers unsealed before then, and she responded, "That would require a judge's decision, and most will not do that. In 41 out of 50 states judges do not overturn adoption decisions."

I struggled to respond, "I have no genetic/blood family. Now that my adopted parents have passed away, I want to learn about my genuine family origins, especially who my real parents are. I may have to hire investigators to help me find them."

I continued, "Why does the government and the legal system make it so difficult to learn about one's family origins?"

In a very caring manner, she educated me: "Mr. Anderson, I know it may seem like these actions are so heartless, but historically they have served a purpose. These rules were created and have been since modified to protect the white and wealthy ruling class. Suppose you located one or both of your parents and their spouse or children knew nothing about your existence. Imagine how much grief and disruption that might cause.

What is most important is that you would have inheritance rights equal to that of the other children, and they may resent you for that. Suppose you then perform a genealogical analysis and learn that some of your history connects you to white families. Should you approach those families? If you are rejected by them should you take legal action, and how many years would that take to resolve?" Is all this headache and heartache worth your continuing to pursue it? Suppose it was revealed that you are a descendent of a family that were slave holders. Can you imagine the potential embarrassment to you and that family?"

My response was resolute, "I am not doing this because I want some material inheritance. More than anything in the world, I just want to meet my mother and hopefully have her hold me. If that happens, I can walk away from this forever. I won't be a problem for anyone, and I really don't care about whether someone who abandoned me feels embarrassed."

Really, I didn't care what anyone in the world felt about my inquiry. As I stood up to leave, she handed me a Kleenex. I did not realize that I had been crying through most of this discussion. I walked out and as I passed others on the street, I noted that they stared at me because I was still crying, and I didn't care. As I walked, I did not hear a sound nor did I notice the congestion of downtown Washington, DC. My skull felt as if it was going to explode as I pondered another critical rejection in my life. I had no plan B, hence I felt more alone and betrayed than ever.

CHAPTER 24
COLLEGE CREATES AN INTELLECTUAL AND A REVOLUTIONARY

When it was time to decide about college, I faced a conundrum. I had several full or partial academic scholarship offers, and I also had several athletic scholarships offers. My dream was to play basketball for Villanova University, but when I discussed this with my parents, I learned that their preference was for me to attend a college/university solely on an academic scholarship.

They feared that I would be perceived as a Negro "jock" on a basketball scholarship wherever I attended, and I would enter a college culture replete with marijuana and Black Nationalism. Hence, I attended the University of Toledo (OH) for my freshman year and majored in Spanish.

In retrospect, this decision did not work well, because this was the first time that I had been separated from the only cultural environment that I had known. Moreover, I became mired in a racist Midwest environment and I hated every day there. The male students of all races from the East coast banded together for protection against the farm boy, Midwest goons. After several clashes with them, I realized that this situation would only escalate, hence I needed to transfer. This meant that I also had to give up my dream of playing basketball there. Little did I realize, that this scenario would be my baptism into the politics of black manhood.

I transferred to Villanova University, but I soon learned that the coach who had recruited me the year before, had moved to another institution. This meant that I did not have a champion to intervene for me within the athletic program and I no longer had a scholarship offer. I was allowed to walk onto the freshman team but for some reason I lost interest in competing. At this level, basketball was a business and no longer fun. I worked hard for two semesters and was able to obtain an academic scholarship.

Another revelation occurred that would direct me to a new path in life. I had become absorbed with the discipline of psychology and I changed my academic major from Spanish to Psychology. I was influenced by the incredible teaching of an instructor, Dr. Aboud, in a Social Psychology course. He and I became very close, and he wanted me to attend graduate school at the University of Missouri, his graduate alma mater, but I decided that I wanted to strive for a Ph.D. program at an Ivy League school. That prestigious institution would turn out to be Cornell University. At the NOVA, my interactions with Dr. Aboud, Dr. Radigan in English, Dr. Carrier in History and African Studies, and Father (Dr.) Hartman in Sociology, laid the groundwork for my future commitment to teaching excellence, and I had a better understanding of why academic rigor was important.

During my tenure at Villanova, I was exposed to a new world of learning, by Dr. Fred Carrier, an avowed Marxist, who taught a course on the History of Africa. It was in that course that I first learned of my origins as an 'African Man' who through historical events had been transposed into an "American Negro." I could not wait for the next class to occur, and in preparation I read everything I could to bolster my identity development. Fred had no idea that he was training a future intellectual revolutionary.

The second person who was influential was, an Augustinian priest and sociology professor. Dr. Frank Hartmann, was a sobering influence on my simmering and emerging nationalism. We talked about national and international events, and especially the condition, and treatment of minorities in this country. I could trust him and the other black students trusted this white priest.

In one course, he told the students that a well-versed person read a major newspaper every day, like the "New York Times," the "Washington Post," or the "Los Angeles Times." Consequently, I had the "Washington Post" delivered to my campus mailbox on a regular basis. Sometimes, I said or did things to Frank just to gauge his response. Once, I walked down to his room in the dormitory, and when he opened the door, I held up a picture of a Playboy centerfold.

I said slyly, "Frank, what do you think of her?"

He laughed and responded: "Not bad, not bad. James, what do you think?"

Through a laugh I retorted, "Frank I like to just mess with you, I know you are a man of God."

Years later, I would work for Frank at the Addiction Services Agency in New York City. I was part of a team of evaluators who assessed the efficacy of drug programs that treated heroin addiction. I learned so much about the culture of heroin addiction and the lethal lure of the drug. My time at that agency allowed me to experience the real underbelly of drug culture.

As time passed, I began to be more involved in both the Civil Rights movement and the emerging Black Nationalist/ Black Power movements on campus and in the city

(Philadelphia). At Villanova, my best friend from high school Cyril, and I, became the co-founders of the Black Student League. Our major goal as a campus organization was to take action to increase the enrollment of minority students at Villanova. We founded a campus newspaper that was separate from the more established periodical, the 'Villanovan.' On the cover of the first publication (of three), I wrote our 'Reason for Being':

Black Wildcat Villanova, Pa –
"A Search For Unity"   *April 23, 1969*

Raison D' Etre
by Jim Anderson

Since this is the initial publication of the "Black Wildcat," we feel that many persons (especially Whites) will misconstrue the purpose or true direction of our newspaper. This misrepresentation of ideas is easily understood as a ramification of the alienation of social groups, hence when Whites read Black material or vice versa, obscurities and partisan responses are to be expected.

The Black Students League at Villanova felt the need to communicate with the general community but primarily the internal and external Black community. Members of the VILLANOVAN (Villanova's predominantly white-oriented newspaper) offered to set aside a special section of their newspaper for the use of the BSL. However, realizing that the Villanovan generally pervades the White community and that its literary freedom is controlled by the VU administration, the BSL decided to create an autonomous publication that would primarily reach the Black community in the area, at other schools, and then, the White community.

The 'Black Wildcat' is neither a revolutionary nor an underground response to our racist society or to Villanova itself, although both may periodically be subjected to vehement degradation, it is not a contemporary commentary on the national and domestic scene, unless issues fall into the arena of Black-White relations; it is not part of the contemporary 'fad' of establishing publications for the hell of it. It is a collection of and an attempted integration of ideas and ideologies taken from the vast reservoir of Black talent that is frequently suppressed within the national and local communications media. It is primarily geared toward educating and unifying Black people by presenting an aggregate of ideas and theories and allowing Blacks to synthesize what they think is functional for their group or community. Secondarily, we are attempting to create an awareness among Whites (not necessarily an understanding of Black theories and idiosyncrasies) that they are being deprived by their own people of hearing the angry responses of Blacks.

The BSL will assume full responsibility for the 'Black Wildcat.' Opinions expressed in the paper do not reflect those of the patrons, of Villanova University, or those of the VILLANOVAN.

Editors-In-Chief..Jim Anderson, Joe Francis
Associate Editors...................................... Farrell Forman, Cyril Crocker
Freshman Class Editor .... Steve Francis
Sophomore Class Editor .... Lamotte Hyman
Contributors..Linda Sims (Immaculata College) Rick Serano (Villanovan), Steve Amadio (Vu)

This First Edition Is Dedicated to Mr. George Raveling Whose Undying Devotion to Villanova and The Black Students Made This Effort A Reality. Good Luck in All You Do, Mr. Raveling. Thank You for Everything.

The Black Student League at Villanova University

I am so proud that the three issues of the 'Black Wildcat' are part of the historical record of Villanova University. Not only was I co-editor of each issue, but I was also the co-founding President of the Black Student League. I was thrust into a major leadership role for the first time, and I became one of the spokespersons for the BSL. Cyril Crocker was the BSL Vice President, and he and I soon became active in the city of Philadelphia. We worked with the city to establish summer camps for poor minority youth in Pottstown, PA. For many of those youths, it was their first time outside of the city proper.

Some of the BSL members worked with the Breakfast Programs in North Philadelphia sponsored by the Black Panther Party. Others worked with gangs that were doing positive things in their community (example, the 12th and Oxford gang). We also provided overnight stays in the dorm, for prospective high school students to encourage them to go to college.

Several members of the Black Student League, also belonged to a predominantly white campus organization, the Social Action Committee (SAC). The two organizations supported mutual goals and our mentors were several Augustinian priests from the Sociology or Theology departments (Father Hartman, Father Ryan, Father Tirrell, and Father Bradly). I can remember being approached one day on campus by a white female, with red hair, who was a member of The Social Action Committee (can't recall her name). She complemented the work of the BSL and noted how our work had awakened her values about an active commitment to service.

We went to lunch a few days later to discuss how the two organizations could work together to accomplish more positive outcomes. I was so moved by her assertiveness, and her initiative propelled me to work harder to bring the races together.

In retrospect, I was becoming a responsible black Man, and a symbol of accountability for the Black Students at Villanova University. I also learned to be more responsible, as I interacted with student leaders from other campuses, and examined their strategic actions, as we became more active in the external community.

As an organization, the BSL sought to expose the white campus community at VU, to prominent black leaders and spokespersons. We were ecstatic when we learned that Muhammed Ali had moved to the Overbrook section of Philadelphia, which was about 10 miles from our campus. One day, Cyril and I decided that we would search for his home so that we could personally invite him to campus as a speaker. We were only aware of the general location of his residence but as campus leaders we were determined to locate it. As we drove around, I noticed that there was one home where a stream of young white kids entered and exited.

I said to Cyril, "I bet that is where Muhammed lives."

We pulled into the driveway and went to the front door and rang the bell.

Muhammed's second wife, Khalilah Ali, answered the door and we explained why we were there. She invited us in and asked us to sit in the living room while Muhammed entertained several white kids by performing magic tricks. She mentioned that Ali loved children and he told the kids in the neighborhood that they could visit at any time. Ali wanted to leave the doors unlocked so they could come in, but she was adamantly against that. Even though their neighborhood was very wealthy, and predominantly White, she still wanted to maintain a sense of privacy. After a period, Ali talked with Cyril and me and committed to speak at Villanova during Black History month. The gymnasium was packed that evening and after his presentation, Ali spent an inordinate amount of time taking questions, signing autographs, and meeting students.

I cannot close out this chapter without narrating one of the scariest and most unsettling racial events in my life. As I indicated earlier, I was politically active while attending Villanova. One summer, I was involved in a voter registration project in West Philadelphia. A colleague and we set up a table outside of the YMCA near 52nd & Sansome streets at their request.

This scenario occurred during the time of a contentious mayoral race. The black community in general had an antagonistic relationship with the incumbent mayor, Frank Rizzo. I guess that Rizzo and his supporters thought that all voter registration projects, were created to encourage blacks to vote him out of office. In fact, we were forbidden from encouraging anyone to vote for a candidate and we never did. One evening, after I finished with registering potential voters, my friend John and I played some basketball at the YMCA. We left there and went by a house, that some black Villanovans were renting. We were sitting in the car talking when suddenly the doors opened, and we were both dragged out onto the ground by a horde of white police.

They proceeded to beat us with night sticks and brass knuckles, and they kept saying, "Now you know what happens to Ni****s who register people to vote against Frank Rizzo."

As you might expect John and I had no idea why this police horde had descended upon us.

We kept screaming, "What did we do, we are not allowed to tell people who to vote for. You must be confusing us with someone else."

John and I were told that we were lying and was handcuffed and thrown into a dark paddy wagon. Inside was a big beefy cop, with a nightstick, who beat us as we were driven to the police station. The neighborhood residents had gathered and began to curse the police and throw stuff at them. Many of those residents belonged to the Nation of Islam.

When we arrived at the Police Station, we were handcuffed to two separate chairs, cursed, and threatened. They told us that they received a report of two guys in a white car selling guns, at the corner of 46th and Woodland Avenues. Supposedly, the information came from an unidentified anonymous caller. I was so angry and physically in pain that I began to curse them. John tried his best to calm me down. John had finished Law School at Villanova, won the moot court competition, and was preparing to take the bar exam.

I was tired of being slapped around and falsely accused, so I said to the two of them and the captain on duty, "Hey you dumb cops imagine how the headline will look in the "Philadelphia Inquirer" newspaper when it reports that two Villanova boys were beaten, detained, and threatened based on false information, and one of the two young men is a graduating law student."

I continued, "I bet there is no tape of an unidentified caller who said we were selling guns. You guys made that shit up as an excuse to beat, arrest, and detain us because I work for the voter registration project. John does not. You are trying to intimidate people who in your eyes, are anti-mayor Rizzo. We are going to sue this precinct to the high heavens."

The three officers then walked to the back and had a brief discussion.

They returned and unlocked our handcuffs and said, "Get the hell out of here, and we better not see you registering voters anymore."

They pushed us out the door and neither one of us had any idea where we were. Later, John and I procured legal assistance from the city's Legal Aid office, but the assigned attorney did not support our case with intensity. After several months, we both realized that our case was being stalled, even though there was no evidence of any phone call that precipitated our beating, and we dropped the case.

I experienced two other disappointments during my undergraduate years at Villanova. One involved racial profiling and the second was a testy situation between the black students and the University president. In the first case apparently, there had been a theft at a jewelry store in one of the small towns that was proximate to the campus (Bryn Mawr). Shortly thereafter, I was called to the Dean of Students office and I was accused of being one of the perpetrators.

Very calmly, I explained that I had spent the weekend with my girlfriend in Philadelphia and on the afternoon when the theft occurred, we were at her mother's house having dinner. I also produced the receipts from the train and subway from my trip into the city. Despite my sources of evidence, Dean B. got angry and shouted at me that I was lying and that he was going to have the campus police escort me to the jewelry store to be identified.

I stood up and said, "I am not going anywhere because I have never been to that jewelry store, and I don't even know where it is. Moreover, you are suggesting that my girlfriend's mother is lying."

At that point, I walked out of his office. I later learned that another VU black student, James B. had also been accused of being my accomplice, and had undergone the same interrogation by Dean B. His alibi was airtight because he had gone home to Washington, DC that weekend.

We both took our case and evidence to Eddie, the African American administrator, who mentored the black students. He took our case to the campus attorney and it was quickly resolved. What we learned from him, was that the robbery did occur and the perpetrators were two black males. The owners of the jewelry store assumed (wrongly) the young men attended Villanova and contacted Dean B. who reviewed the list of Black students and selected the first two names on the list: James Anderson and my friend, James B. The black students on campus were angry about this false accusation and wanted to make a public spectacle of the university. Jamo and I talked about what could potentially emerge as an explosive situation. I did not want to embarrass the university because of the racist actions of Dean B., thus we both decided to put the issue to rest.

In retrospect, it was my love and loyalty for Villanova that prevented me from retaliating through my emerging black nationalism, but I wanted at least an apology from the university which we never received. Dean B. was not given a formal reprimand and continued to occupy his office. I often think back to his arrogance as he thought he could intimidate Jamo and me into confessing. He was more interested in appeasing the concerns of the jewelry store owners.

The second disappointment involved the refusal of the university president, to meet with a representative group of African American students, to discuss plans to increase the number of minority non-athletic scholarships, that could lead to an increase in minority enrollment.

The students decided to stage a sit-in outside of the president's office, and we were joined by some white students. We were there for three days and nights, and the president still would not talk to us. On the fourth day, we learned from one of the campus security officers, that the president had called the State Police to forcibly remove us. I knew that a morally-just demonstration could easily turn into an ugly situation and so, I encouraged the remaining demonstrators to leave the administration building. We asked the priests and administrators that we trusted to intercede on our behalf with the president, but he continued to refuse to meet with us.

Cover of the FSU student newspaper in 2008

CHAPTER 25
WAS I READY FOR THE IVY LEAGUE?

During my senior year at Villanova, I became serious about applying to Graduate School.

I had applied to attend several institutions including Arizona State, Howard University, Morehouse College, and Cornell University. I was rejected by my first choice, Princeton University, and my second choice, University of Michigan. I was disheartened, that is, until my friend, Mel convinced me to visit Cornell University in Ithaca, NY. Within a few days several of us drove to Ithaca, NY.

I was awestruck by the sheer beauty of the campus and the surrounding Finger Lakes region. Literally, this was the most beautiful place I had ever seen. I learned from doing my homework on Cornell University that there was an Africana Research Center, one of the few such centers in the country. There, I met black and African scholars and currently enrolled black graduate students. When I left the center, I walked to the building that housed the Psychology Department, Uris Hall. On my way, I passed lakes, gorges, waterfalls, and the beautiful summer foliage. I talked to the head of the graduate program, who was familiar with my application, and I felt encouraged. By the time I had driven back to my dorm at Villanova, I had made up my mind – I was going to attend Cornell University. I knew that I would miss my Villanova family and the support that I had received during my years there.

My parents were not familiar with the concept of an Ivy League institution; hence they were not being contrary when they pressed me to stay in D.C. and attend Howard University, a historically Black Research university. Once they accepted that I had made up my mind, they supported my decision. I was at a point in my life where I needed a change of scenery. I was ready to leave D.C. and start a new life at Cornell University.

I entered the Ph.D. program in Psychology at Cornell University that fall and within weeks, I learned several things about myself and the university. After two months of attending the assigned courses, it was apparent that the white students in my classes, were more prepared than I was. For example, I struggled in my Advanced Statistics course, because I had never taken an Introductory Statistics course, and the other students had. They also had published articles and worked with researchers at their undergraduate institutions. Again, I didn't have those experiences, hence, I began to study twice as hard.

It was not until I met my first black Professor, A. Wade "Sonny" Boykin, that I had a role model and mentor. He also became a close friend who forced me to understand the rigors associated with being at Cornell.

We also had two other things in common: we both loved playing basketball and loved old Motown and Rhythm and Blues music. I owe so much of my success to him and his rigorous challenge to me to be successful. Wade never let our bond as friends, interfere with his role as a taskmaster with me. A second major thing that I learned was that Cornell University was a hotbed of political activity.

On the east coast Cornell and Columbia University were radicalized. On the west coast, it was UC Berkley and San Francisco State University. I became an active member of the Black Graduate Association, and I hung out with the Black students housed in the Ujamaa dormitory.

I also was stunned by the beauty, intellect, diversity, and political sophistication of the black women that I was now exposed to. Some were undergrads, some graduate students, and some were administrators, but they all were impressive. When they talked about political and historical things that were unfamiliar to me, I realized that I had to step up my game to be respected as a peer. I also developed a distaste for how many black male students, both graduate and undergraduate, disrespected black females on campus. I witnessed several such incidents, but it was my conversations with black females that really informed me how pervasive this situation was. As a result, I met with several black female administrators and suggested that they create a proactive organization that emphasized self-respect for black women, and that they and other sisters serve as mentors for the students. This was the actual announcement on flyers that we distributed on campus:

BLACK SISTERS UNITED (formed in 1974)

There is a new and novel organization forming on campus. It is not designed to be a pressure group or a recreational club. Its primary goal is personal growth. This group is Black Sisters United. It was created a few months ago by women who were tired of the image that black women have in this country. There is ample evidence that the images of black women are often negative and degrading within white and black culture.

In the past this image has been not only psychologically crippling to the black woman, but it is detrimental to the entire race. Surely no people can progress as a group if there is disrespect as a vital element of its constituency. And it is senseless to talk about a collective struggle if the mothers, wives, sisters, and daughters of black men are not treated with dignity. Realizing the ramifications of these negative and unproductive images – dreamed up by the oppressor race, often perpetuated by black men, and reinforced by a minority of black women--several women on campus felt that it was time to get together -- for more than just gossip and fashion shows – to try to deal with the development of their identities.

For too long, black women have been defined by men and consequently have learned to distrust other black women because they view each other strictly as rivals. For too long, Black women have allowed outsiders and pseudo scholars like Daniel Moynihan and other researchers to define what our roles in the Black community are and should be. Black Sisters United advocates that each sister define her own image and role in the struggle.

Black Sisters United will become effective through discussion groups, sensitivity sessions, films (including natural childbirth), panel presentations by Black instructors, administrators and members of the Africana Studies and Research Center. We will schedule a conference sponsored by the Africana Center and Black Sisters United on "The Dimensions of Black Womanhood" with Mari Evans, Barbara Sizemore, Gina Thornton, and Betty Shabazz (the wife of Malcolm X) among others. We will coordinate our activities with other on-campus and off-campus organizations.

In the same way Black people as a race are no longer ashamed to be identified with each other in public, Black women will now identify with each other instead of being competitors.

There is no typical member. All women from all walks of life in Ithaca, NY are encouraged to participate. The organization will include freshman ladies with relationship problems; seniors finding themselves faced with the only alternatives of either a career or marriage; graduate students; professors and staff of Cornell University; staff wives and women of all ages from the Ithaca community. Black Sisters United will cut across generational divides and income gaps since all Black women are keenly aware of their own struggle.

Contrary to popular opinion, Black Sisters United is not equivalent to the typical bra-burning women's' lib type of group bent on pressure politics. Of course, some segments of society and the Ithaca community will see the organization as a threat to their privileged positions. We feel that only those who are taking undue and unfair advantage of the exploitation and oppression of Black women will stand to lose any of their power and privilege. Anyone interested in contacting Black Sisters United may do so by calling either Arlette 256-4131 or Connie 256-3841.

I never thought that I would emerge as a black male feminist, but I guess it was an additive component of my expansion of, and commitment to black nationalism. At Cornell, I was also exposed to individuals on campus and invited speakers, who represented feminism, diversity, and globalism. I remember when Betty Shabazz, Malcolm X's widow, came to campus on three separate visits. After her presentation, she would spend two to three hours talking to a small group of African American students. She was part of the reason that I was motivated to push for the creation of Black Sisters United. She tried to motivate me to either become a Muslim or to join the Nation of Islam, and I graciously declined.

Over the course of time at Cornell, my identity as a graduate student and emerging Black man grew stronger every semester. My identity as an 'African Man,' also blossomed as I interacted more with the professors and students from the Africana Center. I developed a close relationship with an African professor, Dr. Murapa. We played tennis on a regular basis when the weather permitted.

I will never forget that in one of the campus presentations, one of the Africana professors referred to the historical distribution of races in the world as composed of 'People of the Ice' (Europe), 'People of the Sand' (Middle East), and 'People of the Sun' (Africa). I think the professor was John Henrik Clarke. Yes, I realized that this was a simplistic conceptualization of the dispersion of racial groups, but it was included in a broader social-political context, hence it made sense.

Dr. Clarke was attempting to reduce a difficult demographic challenge to a simple visual picture, and what I noted was the power of words to shape the visual images that can influence ideas and belief systems. Later in life, I would utilize this strategy in many of my public academic/research presentations.

Outside of the academic realm the person who had a significant and very profound impact on my life then and now was/is Maurice "Mo" Haltom, my Tai Chi instructor. He was in the same graduate program as I in Psychology. One day as I walked across campus, I saw Maurice leading a small group of students in the practice of some type of slow-moving exercise form. I watched for a while, until my ignorance convinced me to head back to the dormitory. The next time I saw him, I inquired about what I saw him doing that day.

He indicated that it was Tai Chi Chuan, the ancient form of Chinese exercise and self-defense. One of the outcomes of mastering this Asian art, is that it harmonizes the different systems in one's body: the respiratory system, the circulatory system, and the Chi or energy system. Other outcomes include an overwhelming sense of confidence and peace of mind, improved balance, flexibility, and the spiritual feeling of being in harmony with nature. My interest was piqued and I felt there would be little challenge since I always stayed in shape. After all, I was in superior shape due to playing basketball, tennis, jogging, and weightlifting.

Maurice mentioned that he had witnessed how relaxed I played basketball, and tennis, and I would be a good candidate to learn Tai Chi. He asked the students in his Tai Chi classes to think of this art as "Yoga in Motion," that is, it does not emphasize the static stretch positions of yoga, rather it emphasizes continuous motion which promotes an easier flow towards harmonizing our systems.

I agreed to join a beginning class, and I was in disbelief when I struggled to perform the simplest of movements without a consistent degree of stress. To accompany the physical workouts, Maurice required us to read Chinese Philosophy especially the philosophy of Taoism. As time passed, I became an expert at Tai Chi and began to experience the promised benefits. Also, Maurice selected five of the advanced students to learn Tai Chi self-defense, which involved sparring and fighting. And now, forty years later I continually practice the slow form, and I will continue for the rest of my life.

I can vouch for the true existential value of Tai Chi, as it facilitated my ability to cope with periods of significant stress that resulted from: 1) learning that one of my two daughters, Amina, was born mentally challenged due to cerebral palsy, 2) raising Amina alone for fifteen years following a divorce, and 3) the death of my adopted parents in 1994 (6 months apart). During these difficult periods, I increased the frequency of my personal Tai Chi practice, and even taught classes to others. I am sure that Tai Chi helped me to avoid sustained periods of depression, especially after the loss of my adopted parents which left me with almost no family.

I also established close friendships with other Black Graduate students and several Black undergraduates. I developed a primary friendship with a white law student named Terry. He and I are life-long friends who share many similar interests, especially in music. I could write an entire chapter about our individual and joint exploits, but what I most admire about our relationship is that race has never been an issue, in fact it has never been a topic of discussion.

We both loved to play basketball, and when some brothers tried to intimidate Terry, I would intervene on his behalf. The brothers had seen me fight in Tai Chi tournaments, so they were hesitant about taking me on. Terry was raised in Daphne, Alabama, and apparently his love for black music resulted in his immersion in black culture. Terry and Ben B. who is from New York city, both inspired me to succeed academically because they were and are beloved friends who I learned from during our discussions. I have always been impressed by people who could tell me things I did not know, especially items that addressed apolitical issues in the real world. Both also projected a consistent professional demeanor in graduate school, even when circumstances did not require such behavior. The most important aspect of our relationship was that I learned to trust both. This has been the glue that has cemented our relationship for decades.

CHAPTER 26

THE PAST NOW BECOMES THE PRESENT

At the end of my first year at Cornell, I packed up my belongings to drive home to Washington, DC for the summer. The drive normally takes about 6 hours, and I was only thirty minutes outside of D.C., when my car was hit and demolished by an 18-wheel truck. I was thrown from the car at impact, which probably saved my life, because the truck rolled over my car and crushed it. Responsible citizens stopped their cars and sought to lend aid.

I had almost lost consciousness when I heard individuals utter statements like:

"Is he dead?"

"Wipe the blood off his face!"

"Call an ambulance!"

I also heard someone say: "Look at the truck, he is trying to drive away."

At that point I was told that several persons followed the truck on the busy Baltimore-Washington Parkway. Those individuals gave the Maryland State Police the trucking company's name (Hall's), the license number, and the number listed on the large load attached to the cabin. After two weeks of recovery at home and in the hospital, we sought to identify the truck driver that initiated the accident.

My father, an attorney, and I visited the Maryland State Police office several times to no avail. Although they appeared to be helpful, the reality is that they suggested that they did not have enough evidence to identify the truck and driver. Our attorney challenged that position and requested copies of the information that others had given to them. This back and forth reached a point of exasperation until during a final visit, a young state trooper who was white, pulled us aside and said the following:

"I have noted your frequent visits to our office and the frustration you have encountered because they can't locate the truck or driver. I hate to tell you this, but they will continue to act like they are hamstrung. That trucking company has caused so many accidents up and down the East Coast, that they have some type of arrangement with the state police in different states. The other issue is that when the victims of such accidents are Negro, then the efforts to locate the perpetrators is not pursued with much gusto."

I interrupted, "So, everything just gets covered up until people just get tired of pursuing any type of redress."

The trooper responded, "Basically, and I feel so bad for folks like you who get frustrated. If I were you, I would just let it go."

As we drove back to DC, I openly cursed white folks and invoked the specter of racism.

My adopted father was a practicing Christian and he asked me to stop blaming the police because, "They are just trying to do their job," he said.

I realized it was fruitless to continue this discussion with him. Without a car, I decided to take a year off school, and I went to work in New York City for the agency that funded heroin treatment programs throughout the city. I knew about the Addiction Services Agency because it was directed by one of my former professors at Villanova University. He periodically had called me and my best friend Cyril to ask us to come and work for the agency. We accepted his invitation, and we even lived in his apartment for a period, while he crashed with his fiancé.

After a few weeks, Cyril and I noticed that a constant stream of music was emanating from the adjoining condo, and it was disturbing our sleep. I had enough and the next day I told Cyril that after work, I was going to visit our next-door neighbor, and express our frustration with his late-night concerts. I did just that. Before I entered my condo, I knocked on the adjoining door. An African American male opened the door. He had on a baseball cap and dark sunglasses, and both made it hard to see his face. In a very emotional manner, I explained to him the dilemma associated with his playing music late at night and our need to be rested when we went to work every morning. He understood and apologized and stopped playing after 10 p.m.

A few days later, Cyril and I were walking the neighborhood when we met some young professionals and during our conversation, they asked us where we lived.

We told them the address and one of them stated excitedly, "Oh, how is it living next door to the great jazz artist, Miles Davis?"

Suddenly, I was apoplectic and the visage of this man's face became crystal clear to me, even with the sunglasses and baseball cap. I thought, 'How could I have complained about the music of one of the greatest artists ever?' I made it a point to visit Miles the next day. I apologized profusely for suggesting that he should not practice his beautiful art. He laughed and told me not to worry because he recognized that he had been an inconsiderate neighbor. I also apologized for my previous visit during which I referred to his brand of progressive jazz as "sounding like someone playing random notes."

After a year of evaluating heroin treatment programs all over the city, I realized how futile it was to deal with addicts who only lived for the next high, and who would commit any crime to fund their habit. There were not enough treatment programs in NYC to make a dent in that aspect of the drug program. Slowly, I began to realize that it was time to return to Ithaca, and Cornell University. Back at school, I reunited with my friends, reengaged my Tai Chi training, and pursued my graduate work with gusto. I also grew as a committed supporter of different black political and community causes.

I dated a couple of women, but one is etched in memory more so than any of the others. I remember that she was also in another doctoral program in English, and a passionate revolutionary. She was a beautiful woman with long, straight, black hair, and with a wonderful personality that everyone was drawn to. She was an absolute sweetheart. I guess that is why I was shocked when one day, she suggested that we should engage in a demonstrative act of support 'for the international revolution.' I was speechless and decided shortly after, that I needed to end this relationship and I did. She accused me of abandoning her and the movement. Really, freaking really??

It is funny what one thinks about at moments like this, but I kept wondering what my parents would think, when it was reported on the news, that their son had been arrested for committing some revolutionary act.

I decided to reinstate a relationship that I had with a former girlfriend in Philadelphia who I had dated at Villanova. She had become married and divorced since I last saw her, but she ultimately became my wife, the mother of my two daughters, and lived with me in Ithaca, NY. All did not end well between us, but for a period we were deeply in love. She blessed me with two beautiful daughters who have remained the loves of my life. We named our first daughter, Arie and our second daughter, borne four years later, we named Amina. About one year after Amina was born, we learned that she had a condition known as microcephaly and she was in the early stages of cerebral palsy. Both conditions would contribute to a delay in her cognitive development throughout her life. This was a difficult situation to accept for my wife and I, but my training in psychology, allowed me to adapt more quickly. Despite her developmental and physical challenges, Amina was able to exhibit joyful love and affection, especially to her daddy.

I vowed from that point on, that I would make her happy for the rest of her life, since she could not participate in many of the joyful activities that a normal child could experience. I would never abandon her, the way that I was abandoned by my birth parents. Caring for Amina, more than anything else, has elevated my development as a responsible man and father. I also sought to be the same type of father to my other daughter, Arie, but circumstances precluded that from happening until she attended college. I choose not to elaborate on that situation, however, as Arie aged into her thirties, she became more attuned to her role as a part-time caretaker for Amina.

She also became more aware of the relationship between degree attainment and her chosen career pathway which ultimately would become nursing. I am so proud of her discipline and her commitment to help people through their medical problems. Our relationship has matured, and we confide in each other much more than we previously did. She has matured into the role of a proud, responsible, married black woman. I have protected my daughters as any father should and she did the same for her son.

Every male who has dated or married Arie heard this from me, "Arie is a special young woman, and you should treat her in a special way. I know that young couples sometimes have differences, but you two should try to work through any difficulties in a mature and respectful way. However, in a fit of rage, if you choose to curse Arie or, God forbid, if you put your hands on her then I will come for you or I will send somebody to deal with you. Do you understand?"

In every case they stated that they did, but a few looked at me like I was crazy. That was a man-to-man conversation.

I would be remiss if I did not mention three experiences that profoundly impacted my development during my years at Cornell. In the first case, I volunteered to teach a Social Psychology course at Auburn Maximum Security Prison in Auburn, NY. In the second case, I volunteered to serve as a mentor for young males and females on the Onondaga American Indian Reservation. The third case was very different from the first two cases, for it serves as an example of how living in a creative environment, can motivate one to reach beyond his/her own personal expectations. For some reason that I cannot remember, I decided to become a chef and to compete in an annual cooking contest sponsored by the newspaper, the Ithaca Journal.

Teaching Social Psychology at Auburn Maximum Security Prison

As a favor for a friend, I made a commitment to teach inmates for one semester in a night class once a week. I did not realize that simply entering a maximum-security prison entailed a rigorous body search and a thorough examination of all materials that I brought with me. It was also chilling to hear large cell doors close behind me as I made my way to the classroom. As I entered the classroom for the first time, I saw that one prison guard was stationed outside of the door, and another guard stood inside the classroom near the door. I began to reflect on the fact that many of my friends from the Ledroit Park Gang and the Decatur Street Boys were incarcerated in this type of environment at some point in their lives. Thank God, I was not.

The course itself was part of a new state -supported New York Continuing Education Program, and the inmates would receive continuing education credits toward a college degree. Most of the inmates did not have more than a high school education. Although, as I would learn in time, several were avid readers in the prison library. In such a new and unique environment, I had no previous experience, hence, it is understandable that I would make early mistakes, and my first one was a big one. As I entered the classroom, I noticed that the inmates sat by race: Black, White, Native American, and two separate Hispanic groups, with the largest two being the Black, and Latino inmates. Oblivious to prison culture, I sought to apply the same approach that I had utilized as a teaching assistant in my general psychology courses at Cornell.

The prison inmates talked loudly while I was trying to teach, and in my frustration, I said, "Why don't you move around and sit with groups who you may not normally interact with?"

The room fell silent, but each inmate stayed within their own racial group. Suddenly, an inmate decided to school me about prison culture.

As he said dismissively, "Fool, it is obvious that you have never been to prison, cause if you had, you would know about the racial boundaries that define our lives and why they are necessary."

And then, this Caucasian inmate raised his voice and said, as he pointed to inmates in other groups, "I ain't sitting next to any darkies or coons, any spics, or anyone who don't have my back. Only the White Brotherhood has my back."

Seldom am I at a loss for words, but this was one of those moments. I was scared to the core even as the prison guard in the classroom told the inmates to calm down. Members of each racial group were now screaming and cursing one another. It would have been a waste of time to try to teach that night.

The second mistake I made, followed my comments, after they had taken their first exam about four weeks into the course. Damn near all the inmates flunked that exam horribly. As I gave the exams back to each inmate; I said something
that I might have said to undergrads at Cornell, "I don't
know why all of you flunked the exam. I told you I don't grade on punctuation, grammar, or spelling mistakes. I told you folks to just study the content. You have a lot of free time here in prison, so why didn't you use that time to study."

Dead silence fell over the room, until Frank, an older inmate serving two life sentences, spoke up, "Young fella you need to check yourself. Who the hell do you think you are talking to? Gen pop (referring to prisoners housed in the general population in cramped quarters is so noisy that we can't study there, plus, I must watch my back in there."

I apologized profusely and stated that I would work on a different approach to giving exams. By the end of that semester, my nerves were frazzled, but I had a better understanding of prison culture and how far it was removed from the reality of those outside of prison. I also made the critical adjustments in my teaching style to accommodate those who are incarcerated, and it made a difference in their performance.

The next semester I volunteered to teach a general psychology course at an Indian reservation. While I did not make the same mistakes as I did at the prison, I had to learn about Indian culture just as I learned about prison culture. I was also confronted with the visage of third world poverty that I did not expect. Also, there existed the problem of chronic alcoholism.

Since I cooked for the family every day, I decided to upgrade my cooking skills until I could call myself a gourmet chef. After two years of practice, I entered the Annual Cooking Competition sponsored by the local newspaper, the Ithaca (NY) Journal. I submitted two recipes: 1) Just Peachy Curried Rice and 2) Simply Favorable Chinese Chicken. Both were my original creations and I received Honorable Mention status for each one. Not bad, since hundreds of recipes were submitted.

Chapter 27
OTHER SURROGATE MOTHERS

While the nuns and prostitutes occupied a significant role in my life as an abandoned child, there were four other women who shared their time, attention, advice, and motherly love. I would be remiss if I did not pay homage to them.

The first two (Eathel McDaniel and Dr. Betty Cato were present when I was first brought to live with Mr. and Mrs. Anderson, and the latter two existed during my years at Villanova University and Cornell University.

Mrs. Eathel McDaniel

Mrs. McDaniel appeared a few days after the traumatic "Snatch in the Night" that brought me to live with the Anderson's. As a secondary surrogate, she had the longest and strongest tenure in my life, and had the closest relationship with my adopted parents. She seemed to love her role as my surrogate mother and often referred to me as the son she never had (she had no children). A deeply religious woman, Eathel was the spiritual beacon who tried to convince me that the trajectory of my life since birth had been predestined and protected by a higher power. I did not grasp this point until she passed away, and in the vacuum that I experienced, I understood that she had been sent to me by a higher power.

She also tried her best to teach me to read the bible and to explore its mysteries. She deserved 1,000 blessings for such a valiant effort, however, I was resolute in my questioning of its truthful application, to the lives of poor children and women who historically had been global victims, of the actions of men. She became unsettled when I referred to men as "the beasts of history." She also acknowledged that she could not explain why God allowed the ugliness of American slavery or the deadly persecution of the Jews by the Nazi's, or the sexual abuse of children.

What I loved most about Eathel, is that I could confide in her and often benefit from her wisdom, yet she never criticized me for any of my behaviors, some of which I was embarrassed to share with her. As a surrogate parent, she chose to spend the remaining years of her life, showering me with her love, and in return I took care of her financially. No matter where I lived and worked, I made it a point to visit her as often as I could. As she was nearing death, she gave me something that I will treasure the rest of my life. It is a very simple laminated, letter-sized sheet that contained the following statement:

~Son~
You Are Loved ~For the Little Boy You Were...
The Special Man You Are Now...And the Wonderful Son
You Will Always Be.

When she passed away, I was crushed. She left instructions for me to say some words at her funeral and I struggled to get through the ceremony. I spoke of how proud she was of me and my academic and professional achievements and she shared that with many other individuals.

I am absolutely convinced that this angel was sent to me by a higher power.

Dr. Betty L. Cato (Strudwick)

The second woman who had a significant role in my life, after I was delivered to the home of Mr. and Mrs. Anderson against my will, was Dr. Betty Cato. Apparently, since I had no real parents, then I did not have the requisite medical inoculations that should have occurred, during my childhood. Shortly, after my arrival at the Anderson residence. I contracted a near-fatal case of rheumatic fever. Dr. Cato was a pediatrician who had a home office that was located diagonally across from the Anderson residence. She and her husband, Dr. Warren Strudwick, attempted to treat me as I became progressively worse, and then the 'Miracle on Jefferson Street' occurred (Chapter 16).

Subsequently, Dr. Cato and I developed a close relationship, as she continued to serve as my personal pediatrician, far beyond the normal age, that young adolescents transition to being treated by a general physician. As I grew older, I refused to transition from her care until I reached high school, and it was often embarrassing to sit in the waiting room, of her office, with young children and their parents, who often commented to Dr. Cato about treating a teenager. At this point, Dr. Cato suggested that I enter the back door to her office whenever I had an appointment. I did this for several years until she suggested that I transition to her husband's care.

Why did I choose to be in her care for so long? The answer is quite simple to me. Desperate for a mother-figure, she endeared herself to me as she treated me without judgement, through my fears of being brought to a new environment to live, and through my brush with death.

Dr. Betty L. Cato, was a legendary pediatrician to generations of families, mostly Black, in the Washington, DC area for 45 years. In 1958, she and her husband, Dr. Warren Strudwick, helped to integrate Washington, DC hospitals, which until that point, would not treat Black patients nor train Black doctors. When I learned recently, that she passed away peacefully at home on February 1, 2022, I burst into tears uncontrollably. I had not seen her for nearly 58 years and scenes from my past with her flooded my consciousness. I am alive today because of her, and she will always be my beloved Dr. Cato.

Abigail "Moms" Pankey

At Villanova University, I met several students who were siblings and who lived in West Philadelphia. Over time I grew very close to this wonderful family, the Pankey's. One daughter, Marian, always referred to me as her brother. Over time my roommate and best friend, Cyril, also established a relationship with the family which led to our first invite to the Pankey's home for dinner. Walking into the residence, I noted the presence of many children, and I had no idea of who they all belonged to.

The highlight of that Sunday was meeting the family matriarch, Abigail "Moms" Pankey. She was the consummate single mother, neighborhood organizer, community politician, and overall sweetheart. Before Cyril and I left that evening, I had fallen in love with Moms. From that point, on she looked after Cyril and me. She made sure we had summer jobs and, frequently, a good meal. One of her daughters who attended Villanova, had a young son named Chipper and he and I grew very close. I recognized that he was absent a caring father figure and so whenever possible, I would shower my attention upon him. I was distraught to learn years later, that he had been sentenced to a long prison term. Despite the love, attention, and security that he received at home; Chipper was swallowed up by the mean streets of Philadelphia.

After many interactions with her, Moms became my surrogate mom. When I could not see her, I called her on a regular basis just to check in. I grew to respect her as stalwart in her community and she ruled her household with a firmness that belied a loving heart.

She had such a sweet way of saying my name, "Jimmy." Often when I would visit, I could see how weary Moms was, but she forced herself to act upbeat so as not to disappoint me. Disappoint me? I had long been aware of her tireless struggle to simultaneously bring stability to her home and community. In return, it was clear that everyone loved and respected her, but the real support that she needed was not always there. Cyril and I decided that one way that we could reciprocate her selfless love for us was to take her to an elegant restaurant. We selected a Chinese restaurant on City Line Avenue, located in one of the nicer sections of Philadelphia. She genuinely enjoyed herself and shared with us that she could not remember the last time that someone had taken her to dinner. I should have done more to assist Moms in her life's journey, just as she sought to assist and provide for everyone.

When Moms passed away, I was alerted to the funeral arrangements in Philadelphia. I arrived at the church almost 2 hours before anyone else and positioned myself next to her open casket so I could gaze at her and talk to her. I did not want her to be alone before her family and friends arrived. It was the least I could do since, in her lifetime, Moms was always there for me. Moms, I miss you terribly, and the world has lost much of its luster and tries to function absent your love. I will never forget that, as you were nearing death, you phoned me to tell me that you loved me and considered me your son.

Marilyn D. Hayes

During my early undergraduate years at Villanova University, the institution did not provide on-campus living arrangements for females. The university was co-ed but there was a clear absence of females of color. Hence, the brothers on campus had to find other ways to meet and date sisters, and that often meant that we had to travel to other campuses to court a young lady. I only seriously dated two young Black women while at the NOVA and both attended other institutions (Immaculata College and the University of Pennsylvania.

I met Elaine at an off-campus party that was attended by several brothers from the NOVA and among the females present, were several from the University of Pennsylvania. She and I dated and ultimately our relationship became serious enough that she asked if I would like to meet her mother. I said yes, and a Sunday dinner was arranged. The visit was to take place in North Philadelphia at 21st and Lambert Streets where her mom lived. After a train ride into the city, and a bus ride to North Philly, I then began the walk to her mom's residence. About every two blocks, I was stopped by a group of Black youth, who asked where I was from and where was I going.

Little did I know, that I was in serious gang territory and these dudes were protecting their turf. My identity as a Villanova boy, seemed to make me harmless to them, and probably saved me from a royal ass-whipping or worse. Finally, I arrived at Elaine's house to meet her mother and within the first 15 minutes, I realized that her mom was a smart, no-nonsense woman hence I didn't waste time trying to charm her. I told myself, "No mistakes," just get through this first meeting. When dinner was ready, her mom indicated that I should go upstairs to wash my hands. I promptly did that but as I walked in and out of several rooms, I could not find a bathroom with a hand basin. I then walked downstairs and expressed my dilemma to them. They both laughed and indicated that they washed their hands in the bathtub. They teased me about being a spoiled young man who came from a home with multiple bathrooms each with its own hand basin. They were unaware of the poverty associated with my life scenario before I met the Andersons.

After that first meeting, I realized how much I liked her mom (Marylin), and as time passed, we became fonder of each other. She was still no-nonsense, but she laughed more and I gradually became more open. I was happy when she moved from Lambert Street to a much nicer and safer area of Philadelphia. My relationship with Marilyn and her daughter provided me with a sense of belonging and feelings of being loved and cared for – necessities that were absent for most of my life.

Unfortunately, an event occurred that caused Elaine and I to dissolve our relationship and to lose contact. The void in my life existed once again and I was flooded with the series of emotions that had haunted me most of my life: abandonment, depression, disillusionment, compartmentalization, and a loss of faith in love, myself, and God.

After thirty plus years of no contact at all with Marilyn (or Elaine), I moved to Texas to take a position at Texas A&M University. Imagine my surprise, when I was contacted one day by Elaine, who had read an announcement about my appointment. Elaine, her husband, and mom now lived in

Houston and, once again, I was reunited with Marilyn. I have visited her several times and we talk on the phone periodically, especially on her birthday. I am thrilled when she ends our phone conversations by telling me that she loves me. In terms of her age, she is well into her 90's and I know she will leave me soon. I am trying to prepare for that inevitable day when another surrogate mother exits my life – a son once again will lose his mother.

PROLOGUE

I never thought that writing a memoir could leave one mentally and emotionally exhausted. Practically speaking, why should events that happened several decades ago have such a profound personal impact? Throughout the memoir, I describe multiple traumatic events that have fueled the content and context of my historical memories.

My original intent was to be as objective and descriptive as possible, but in a short period of time, I realized that was impossible. To simply state that I was abandoned at birth by my parents without attaching the historical results of that trauma to my life would not account for the evolution of the person I am today. Thus, I often become frustrated by caring individuals who have said to me,

"James, can't you just forget or put aside those things that have caused you so much emotional pain? It seems like an obsession for you."

As a professional psychologist, I recognize why such statements are made. Friends who care about me and love me do not want me to suffer, but they also are naïve as to the power and impact of my life experiences. While I limited this memoir to my pre professional years (birth to 29 years old), I am cognizant that my professional career and related personal life were also deeply affected by early emotional traumas. I chose to emphasize those formative years of my personality development, which provided the emotional resilience and strength that I needed in my professional career.

I began this memoir with a quote from a reporter who interviewed me during my tenure as a Vice President and Associate Provost at the State University of New York at Albany. I will close with a poem about me produced by a nationally, recognized, distinguished African American professor who was also at University of Albany, SUNY. To a great degree, it represents how significant, emotional events that occur early in one's life, can contribute to strength and success in adulthood.

The poem also references the most significant mentor and advocate in my life who is deceased, Dr. Kermit Hall. Following Dr. Hall's tragic passing, I chose to leave the university, and the poem was written around that time. I respected and loved Dr. Hall and his spouse, Phyllis, immensely and I could not continue at that institution without them. In Dr. Slade's eyes, the lifelong evolution of my emotional resilience contributed to my success as a Vice President and Associate Provost at SUNY-Albany.

This poem represents a tribute to those individuals who invested in me, saw promise in me, sacrificed for me, and who dared to love me and care for me. I have evolved into a successful Black man and Dr. Slade captures this growth in his poem.

DR. JAMES ANDERSON
By Leonard A. Slade, Jr. (2008)

Daily we think of you
at the university: more
conscientious than many
of us, your teaching us
how to raise academic standards. Everywhere
on our campus you
are affectionately called "The
Fix It Man," because no problem
is too complex for you to solve.
"The evidence is here," as you remind us how
it's done to take students under your intellectual
wings and soar with them to
fulfill dreams. And now we
really appreciate what you've
done for the institution we love
and ask that you honor the memory of President
Hall by helping us all build a greater University,
where your friends ardently support you and
your family, for "the evidence
is here" that this place desperately needs you
where students call you
"The Bomb" and where President Hall would
smile in the Heavens knowing that you are
doing His work, singing.

Photo Courtesy of Best Perspectives Photography

Photo Courtesy of Best Perspectives Photography

Photo Courtesy of Best Perspectives Photography

DR. JAMES A. ANDERSON

is the former Chancellor and Professor of Psychology at Fayetteville State University (2008-2020). He previously served at SUNY Albany, Texas A& M University, North Carolina State University, Indiana University of Pennsylvania and Xavier University of New Orleans. He is the author of the book: *"Driving Change Through Diversity and Globalization – Transformative Leadership in the Academy,"* and he edited the book: "The Unfinished Agenda of Brown V. Board of Education." He also has published numerous book chapters and journal articles. He has served as a consultant for the accrediting body, SACSCOC. He holds an undergraduate degree from Villanova University, and a Ph.D. in psychology from Cornell University. He was born and raised in Washington, DC. He served on the Board of Trustees at Villanova University for two 5-year terms, and he continues to serve on the Board of Directors for CASL (Center for the Advancement of STEM Leadership), the Board of Directors for the North Carolina History Center on the Civil War, Emancipation, and Reconstruction, and the Board of Trustees for St. John's College Prep High School, and the community organization of 100 Black Men. He is also a member of the oldest professional fraternity for Black Men, Sigma Pi Phi.